BILLION TO ONE

A Memoir

WINNING THE $50 MILLION LOTTERY HAS ITS PRICE

By Randy Rush
with Ingrid Ricks

13 Billion to One
Copyright © 2020 Randy Rush

First Edition, Collector's Copy

Paperback ISBN: 978-1-9992524-0-3
Hardcover ISBN: 978-1-9992524-1-0
Ebook ISBN: 978-1-9992524-2-7

ALL RIGHTS RESERVED

No part of this book may be reproduced in any form—electronic, mechanical, or with any other means, including photocopying—without the author's written permission, except in the case of brief quotations embodied in critical articles or reviews.

Written by Randy Rush with Ingrid Ricks

Published by Rantanna Media Inc.
rantannamedia.com

Design by Rainy City Productions
rainycityproductions.com

Image Credits: All images provided by Randall Rushs, unless otherwise specified.

Author's Note:

Some names have been changed for privacy reasons. All currency unless otherwise noted is in Canadian Dollars.

Dedication

This book was the result of the hard work by many people, especially Ingrid Ricks who did the writing and editing and whose inspiration was truly unparalleled in my life before this project.

To Conway Kitty. For just being there.

And most of all the Creator the great I AM, the Alpha and Omega, the Source of all life.

Prologue

November 1, 2015

My attorney's words swept through me, triggering a tidal wave of panic and rage.

"We have got to talk, Randy," he said, the color gone from his face. "We've got big problems."

I could feel my legs trembling, my hands balling into fists.

I knew it.

I had known it ten days earlier during my drive to Scottsdale. It's why I had put together an impromptu business team and flown them all to Arizona. I needed professionals who could help me get to the bottom of everything before it was too late.

Anger surged through me as I continued to take in my attorney's words. "Mike and I finally managed to corner Jeremy and ask about your assets and money. Jeremy says it's all his. He says you have nothing."

Those last words knocked the air out of me. I was so stunned that for a minute, I couldn't speak. What did he mean it was all HIS? I put up the $4.6 million investment. It was my money—all of it.

My eyes flew across the rooftop deck of the W Hotel, searching the throngs of people for the scumbag who thought he could steal my money. My stomach clenched each time my eyes landed on yet another person enjoying a $15 cocktail while feasting on overpriced finger foods. Who were these people anyway? They certainly weren't Justin Timberlake, Taylor Swift, or the other celebrities I was told would be attending the company launch party. They were likely freeloaders who had been rounded up off the street to enjoy the party I was footing.

Before I could locate him, Jeremy was standing next to me. His eyes were bloodshot and bugging out of his head.

"Great party, huh, Randy?" he said, moving his face close to my ear.

I dug my fingernails into my palms to keep from breaking his legs.

"It's okay," I replied, forcing my voice to stay measured. I knew if I lost control of myself, there was no turning back.

I must have hit a nerve because his face immediately turned red and the veins in his neck looked like overblown balloons ready to pop.

"What do you mean? I think it's awesome."

He leaned in closer. "What are you guys f@#%ing doing? You're running around the party talking business and putting a downer on the whole thing."

Now it was everything I could do to keep from breaking both his arms and his legs.

"Pardon me?" I snapped back. "What did you just say to me? I would never talk to you in those terms and you won't talk to me in those terms. You've been told and warned."

My tone was still measured, but there was a lethal edge to it.

Jeremy took a step back.

"You're done, Rush," he snarled before slinking back into the safety of the crowd. "I'm finished with you."

Every nerve in my body was burning, but before I could scream, "Jeremy, you're fired!", chase him down, and shove him into the rooftop pool, my friend Trevor intervened.

"Come on, Randy, let's go," he urged. "Let's figure out how to get this piece of scum."

I forced my legs to follow him to a hotel conference room that Mike had just secured so we could regroup and come up with a game plan.

I felt like I was sinking, as though I had stepped into a pool of quicksand and was already in too deep to get out.

Why hadn't I listened to my gut? Why had I been such a fool?

The red flags and warning signs from the previous five months began flashing through my mind: Jeremy's new Ferrari and Porsches, his ongoing pressure for more money, the repeated lies and stonewalling when my team had asked basic questions about company operations and finances.

My thoughts fueled my rage, but they also ignited an intense pain inside of me. It was one thing to be taken by a stranger, but quite another to be so personally betrayed by people I considered family.

It was because of my love for Dave that I had even agreed to meet with his son, let alone trust him enough to invest $4.6 million in his technology business venture. Now it was clear that Dave and his wife, Shirley, were not only aware of their son's intentions, they were in on it.

I paced the room as my newly assembled business team began mapping out a legal strategy to regain my assets and money. I could hear the company launch party continuing on the rooftop deck—the music being blasted by the DJ who had been flown in from Toronto for the evening and the muffled laughter between songs.

Rage once again took over, permeating every inch of my

body. I was going to make everyone who was involved in this in any way pay. I didn't care how long it took, or how much money I'd have to spend on legal fees and investigative research. I was going to get justice. And it started with ending the gravy train for my one-time friends.

I grabbed my cell phone and pounded out the message I couldn't wait for Dave and Shirley to read.

"As soon as you are back in Canada, I want the two of you to pack your things and get out of my house," I typed. "Your son just ripped me off for $4.6 million and I want you gone."

1

January 31, 2015

My brain froze as I counted the zeros flashing across the lottery-ticket scanner screen.

I knew seven was a lot. But between the sudden shock and adrenaline rush, I was having a hard time remembering just how many zeros constituted a million dollars.

The words "You've Won" ricocheted through my body as I stared at the screen, counting and recounting the zeros lined up next to a dollar sign and the number five.

Seven zeros. Eight numbers including the number five. Was it really telling me I had just won FIFTY MILLION DOLLARS?

I could hear my heart pounding as I rescanned the lottery ticket. I knew this had to be a malfunction, some sort of scanner error. But when I scanned the ticket a second time, the same eight numbers appeared with the "You've Won" message.

"Filina, I think I've won fifty million dollars!" I heard myself screaming to the store clerk, the only other person around. "Seriously. I think I've WON!"

Rocket fuel shot through me, propelling my body toward the front of the small, corner grocery store. I locked the door and flipped the Open sign to Closed. Then I was back at the checkout counter, shoving the ticket in front of her.

I heard her breath catch as she took in the numbers and compared them with the winning numbers from the Lotto Max drawing two weeks earlier. Unbeknownst to me, a single ticket holder had won the jackpot, but the winner had yet to come forward.

"Oh my gosh, Randy, you've won!" Filina exclaimed. "You've hit the jackpot!"

Now we were both screaming, and I was on such a high I was having a hard time controlling my body. Sheer excitement sent me flying up and down the aisle, shouting, skipping, jumping. Then I was back at the counter.

"What do I do?"

Every nerve in my body was tingling. I was sweating and my hands were trembling. I had trouble breathing.

"You've got to sign it," Filina said, pushing a pen toward me. "That way, no one can take it from you."

I grabbed the pen, scribbled my name on the signature line, and felt sick.

"Oh, no," I yelled. "I signed Randy Rush and my legal name is Randall Rush. What if that invalidates it?"

In my forty-eight years on the planet, I'd had enough life experience to know that if something could go wrong, it WOULD go wrong. And I was holding a piece of cardboard paper representing fifty million reasons for things to go terribly wrong.

Filina, who had calmed down by now and taken charge of the situation, assured me I would be fine. She asked if she could run my ticket on her scanner behind the checkout counter to see if the Big Winner red flashing light and siren would go off. Within seconds, the siren sounded and the red light began flashing. It was like we were at a carnival.

We both let out another celebratory scream. Once again, I was bouncing from one end of the corner grocery store to the next. I knew this had to be a dream, but it felt so real I didn't want to wake up.

"What do I do now?"

I had never hyperventilated before, but given my rapid breathing and raging heartbeat, I was sure that was what was happening.

"Now we've got to phone it in," she replied.

I struggled to control my breathing and keep my feet pinned to the ground as I listened to her dial the number to the Lottery Call Center in Winnipeg and calmly explain that she was calling from Lamont Grocery to report a $50 million jackpot winner.

After a minute, she turned the phone receiver over to me.

"Good afternoon, sir," a woman's voice said. "Congratulations."

I could feel my throat muscles constricting and heard Filina's voice urging me to breathe as the call center operator began rattling off a series of verification questions. She asked me my name, where I lived, and when and where I had purchased the ticket. She also had me read the security number off the ticket and then put me on hold so she could run some security checks on her end—including viewing surveillance video—to corroborate the information I'd provided.

"Just breathe," Filina instructed again as I clung to the phone, waiting for the security checks to be completed. "It's going to be fine."

After three or four minutes that lasted an eternity, the woman's voice was back.

"You are now the registered winner," she announced. "It's

official."

She told me the next step was to report with my ticket to the Western Canada lottery commission office in St. Albert, located about ten minutes north of Edmonton, on Monday morning.

"Congratulations," she repeated before ending the call.

I handed the phone receiver back to Filina. I was so revved up I couldn't speak. I locked my eyes on the checkout counter, trying to steady myself and process what was happening. That's when I noticed the stack of premium, soft-serve cat food cans I had placed there a few minutes earlier and remembered why I had ventured out into two and a half feet of snow and -22°C temperatures in the first place: My cat, Conway Kitty, was out of soft cat food.

It was a typical frigid winter Saturday in Lamont, a sleepy suburb located about forty miles from Edmonton. I had slept in late and enjoyed a lazy morning puttering around my house with a large mug of coffee. But by early afternoon, Conway's angry meows and deadly glares had escalated to the point they could no longer be ignored.

"Okay, I'm going," I growled back at my twenty-seven-pound cat.

I reluctantly pulled on my snow boots, threw on my parka, and grabbed my truck keys to make the half-mile drive to the corner grocery. As I was heading out the door, I noticed a stack of lottery tickets I had accumulated and grabbed those, too, figuring I would check them while at the store.

That was less than an hour ago. But now it seemed like another lifetime.

I was still so high on endorphins it was hard to think straight. But as I paid for the cat food, paranoia swept through me.

What was I going to do between now and Monday morning? I was holding a lottery ticket worth $50 million. FIFTY

MILLION DOLLARS! Lamont was a small town and word always spread fast. *What if someone tried to steal it from me?*

My thoughts ping-ponged from one horrifying scenario to the next. Some of them ended violently, and all of them ended with my $50 million lottery ticket being peeled out of my hand.

As it now stood, Filina was the only person in town who knew about the win. And I had to keep it that way.

"Promise me you'll say nothing to anyone until Monday morning," I said, my voice half demanding, half pleading. "If you do that, I'll come back and compensate you generously."

I could see the surprise on Filina's face. She was a good person, and I knew from our past conversations that she had a hard life.

"Randy, I promise I won't say a word," she assured me.

She paused for a minute before continuing.

"The only thing I want is a small trailer to put on my parents' property so I have a place to live," she said. "I'm staying with them so I can take care of them, but there's not enough room for me."

"Done," I replied.

I left the store, waded through the snow back to my work pickup truck, climbed in, and quickly locked the door. It was so cold I could see my breath, but I was on such a high I couldn't feel anything but my heart pounding against my chest.

I turned my key in the ignition and cranked up the heat, but I was too amped up to drive. My body was buzzing with electricity and the sound of a voice that grew louder with each word. "You've just won fifty million dollars!" it boomed. "You are LOADED!"

2

It was my friend Daryl who convinced me to start playing the lottery.

We were kicking back with a couple of beers at his house one Sunday afternoon, watching an Edmonton Eskimos football game, when seven numbers flashed through my mind.

The numbers were so vivid it was as though someone had placed them on flash cards in front of me. Each number was outlined in a gold border, with a red border encasing the gold. It was so surreal that I mentioned it to Daryl.

"Dude, that's weird," he replied. "You should write them down."

He handed me a notepad so I could scribble out the numbers before I forgot them.

"Those look like great lottery numbers," he observed as he looked them over. "You ought to start playing."

I immediately shut him down.

"I don't play the lottery," I replied. "That's a waste of money."

Daryl laughed.

"Yeah, but wouldn't it piss you off if those numbers won?"

He had a point. And there was something else. Several years earlier I had connected with my dad's mother, Grandma Hazel, and we had discovered a mutual love for the game of cribbage. We were in the middle of the card game and I had just discarded two cards. I needed a seven to get to twenty-four, one of the highest hands possible. Just as I went to cut the cards, Grandma Hazel put her hand on mine.

"My crib," she barked. "Get your hands off my cards."

The second she touched me, a seven of hearts flashed through my mind, encased in the same red and gold that bordered the numbers I had just seen. When the card flipped over, it was a seven of hearts. It had scared the crap out of me back then. But now, given the similar bizarre incident, it seemed like a sign.

After that day, I began playing the lottery and had done it steadfastly for the past eight years. I invested only $20 to $25 a week, often playing the $3 cards that always included my numbers and came with a couple of computer-generated quick picks. It was one of those quick picks that had actually hit the jackpot. But if it hadn't been for my numbers, I would have never started playing.

I decided to share the news with Daryl first.

With the heat now blasting through my truck, I hit his contact number and waited.

Daryl answered on the third ring. The endorphins were still shooting through me at such a rapid pace that for a few seconds, I had a hard time getting the words out. When I finally did, I was almost incoherent.

"Daryl! I've won! I've won! I've won!"

"What are you talking about?" he asked, clearly confused by my gibberish.

I inhaled a few mouthfuls of the heated air now blowing through the cab of my pickup, hoping I could slow my breathing and thoughts enough to make my words audible.

"Remember those numbers—the numbers you said sounded like great lottery numbers?" I managed. "I've hit the jackpot!"

Daryl, who had been on the receiving end of my jokes before, wasn't having any of it. "You are so full of it," he replied, clearly annoyed at having his Saturday afternoon interrupted.

I knew how it sounded. I would have had the same reaction. But I was ready to burst and needed someone I trusted to help me process this news.

I bit my lip to ground myself and tried again.

"Daryl, would I phone you up on a Saturday afternoon and lie about something like this?"

Maybe it was my halted breathing or the urgency in my tone. Whatever it was, my words finally penetrated.

"No," he admitted. "You wouldn't do that."

I could now hear curiosity in his tone and wanted to drag out the suspense by making him guess the number. But I couldn't hold it in.

"Dude, I've won fifty million dollars!"

There was silence. Then Daryl let out a whoop! "Holy s@#!, man. Unbelievable!"

The next call I made was to my friend Brent, who lived in Ottawa. The two of us had met the summer before fourth grade at a neighborhood park in New Westminster, a rough, working-class town located about forty-five minutes from Vancouver. We were both skinny and on the short side. But Brent was as tough as they got. He was the kid that no one wanted to mess with—no matter how big they were. I was more of the class clown with the big personality. But I knew how to use my fists and wasn't scared of a fight, and the two of us became instant friends. In many ways, our home lives mirrored each other. Like my mom, Brent's mom was young and single. And like me, Brent was an only child.

Though my mom—who was constantly moving us from one apartment to the next—relocated us after the school year ended, our friendship stuck, and Brent was as close to a brother as it got.

He now held a prominent position as a senior officer for the Royal Canadian Mounted Police, but he and his wife had triplets to support and I'd been trying to convince him to play my numbers ever since they had flashed through my mind.

"I'm telling you, these numbers are going to hit," I reiterated numerous times over the years. Each time, he either shrugged or laughed it off.

Brent's wife, Kim, answered the phone and told me they had company.

"It doesn't matter," I replied. "It's important and I need to talk with him now."

As soon as Brent was on the line, I told him to head to his bedroom so he could be alone.

"Are you sitting down?" I asked.

"Yes. What's up?"

I knew I was acting strange, and I could hear the concern in his voice.

"Remember those numbers I told you to play?" I blurted. "I hit the jackpot—fifty million dollars!"

Both of us had a cutting sense of humor and had engaged in plenty of back-and-forth bantering over the years. But we had also shared plenty of serious moments and I could almost hear him trying to decipher what this was.

"You're kidding, right?" he finally responded.

I knew it sounded like BS. I was still having a hard time believing it myself. But if it was a dream, it was so real that I had to go with it.

"Brent, would I interrupt your company if I was kidding?"

By the time I hung up with Brent, I had calmed down

enough to consider driving home. I made a couple more quick calls to other close friends and then started up the engine.

I didn't know what to do with myself. Excitement collided with fear and paranoia. I parked my truck, sprinted into the house, and bolted the lock behind me. Then Conway's belligerent meows reminded me why I had gone to the store in the first place. I grabbed a can of the soft-serve cat food and headed to his bowl.

"Conway, I've hit the jackpot!" I told him as I scooped out his food. "I've won FIFTY million dollars! We're loaded!"

I was climbing the walls, pacing from one room to the next. I was so pumped up my entire body felt like it was going to explode. But Conway couldn't care less. He had his face buried in his bowl and was chowing down the food, oblivious to the fact that he could now have a gold-plated bowl and as much gourmet, soft-serve cat food as he could devour if he played his cards right.

I took a seat next to him on the floor, running my hands through his thick, white and gray fur as he ate. I knew he was smart; he was a purebred Maine Coon and they were known for their intelligence. But it was clear he wasn't understanding the magnitude of what had just happened to me.

Another emotion began seeping through me, mixing with my euphoria and paranoia: loneliness. I usually didn't mind being alone. But I was experiencing the biggest day of my life—the biggest day of several lifetimes—and aside from my friends and a cat who wasn't interested, I had no one to share it with.

I had always planned to get married and start a family. But I hadn't yet met the person I wanted to spend my life with. I had grown up an only child of a teen mom who now lived in the Czech Republic with my stepdad, Steve. We'd been estranged for nearly two years, and, aside from a half-sister I'd met only a few times in my life, I had no family.

My friends must have sensed my need for company because within a half-hour of being home, first Daryl, and then another friend, called to say they were on their way.

The three of us spent the afternoon and evening drinking single malt scotch while catching up.

"Fifty million dollars! Holy crap!" one of us would holler every now and then, causing an eruption of cheers and toasts. Then we would get back to enjoying each other's company.

It was past midnight by the time our impromptu party wrapped up. I was buzzed from the alcohol and exhausted from my day, but I couldn't turn off my mind.

I was a multimillionaire! A fifty-million-dollar millionaire. It was so big I couldn't wrap my head around it. In a few days, according to the call center operator, I would have a lump sum, tax-free deposit of $50 million wired to my bank account.

The endorphins were going full speed again, and my heart was beating so hard it felt like it could beat a hole right through my chest.

I resisted the urge to run through my neighborhood shouting the news. Instead, I pulled out a comforter and pillow from the den closet and took my familiar spot on the couch. I stretched my body and closed my eyes, hoping I could at least relax a little. But every cell in my body was awake and on steroids.

Images of stacks of cash floated through my mind. I was floating, too—sometimes bumping into the ceiling above me, other times flying through space. My attention deficit disorder was on full throttle. I jumped from one surreal scene to the next: picking out a fully-loaded Porsche from the nearby dealership, sitting on the balcony of a five-star hotel overlooking the beaches of the French Riviera, chartering a luxury jet for an around-the-world trip with friends.

FIFTY MILLION DOLLARS! It was so much money I

couldn't even envision it. It was a ton of money. Literally.

My head was spinning. I needed to settle down, to concentrate and organize my thoughts. I relaxed my eyes again and willed myself to focus on the mental to-do list I had started developing in preparation for this day.

As far-fetched and crazy as it sounded, I had known in my gut that I would hit the jackpot. The feeling had intensified over the past couple of years, and the energy coming at me had been so powerful that I sometimes lay awake at night making plans for my inevitable win.

The first item on my post-win to-do list was to get out of Dodge. Lamont was such a small town that everyone knew everyone, and I knew I would be an easy mark. I had heard enough lottery-winner horror stories to know that people would immediately start hounding me for money, and I needed to get someplace where no one knew me.

In my "What to Do When I Win the Lottery" planning sessions, I played around with different sums of money, ranging from $1 million to $5 million. If I won $1 million, I figured I would have enough money to buy the sports car of my dreams, pay off my house, and hire someone to live there and watch over Conway while I enjoyed a year off of work to travel. If I won $5 million, I would have enough money to retire. In that case, I planned to immediately quit my job, purchase another house in a different part of Canada, and then travel freely around the world while figuring out my next steps. That's as far as I had gotten. None of my pre-win preparations had ever considered a $50 million scenario.

Conway meowed and jumped onto the sofa. I shifted to make room for him on my pillow, which he was convinced belonged to him.

I smiled as Conway snuggled up against me, his long, shaggy fur warming the side of my face. This couch had been our spot since I had picked him up as a five-month-old kitten from his breeders in Alberta three years earlier. Not everyone was a fan of our sleeping arrangement. I could still hear the annoyance in my ex-girlfriend's voice when she confronted me about it.

"Randy, you make more than $200,000 a year," she had fumed. "Why don't you have a bed?"

I eventually relented and purchased a bedroom set, complete with a king-sized bed. But most of the time I slept on the couch. The reality was that sleeping on the couch was much more than a habit for me—it was an emotional symbol from my past.

My thoughts drifted to that other couch that I had slept on twenty-two years earlier: a worn, gold-colored, paisley-patterned couch that provided a refuge when I was at the lowest point in my life.

I had never understood what drove people to commit suicide until the night I considered it for myself. It was past midnight and I was standing on a dark bridge in New Westminster, staring down at the water below and wondering if jumping would help end the pain.

Suffocating despair had closed in so tight on me that I couldn't see a way out. I was twenty-six years old and had nothing: no career, no job prospects, no relationship, no money, no apartment, no place to go.

A couple of months earlier, I had lost my job as a sales rep due to territorial cutbacks. The economy was so bad I was striking out on every position I applied for. It had gotten so dire I'd been forced to go on welfare and move back in with my mother and stepdad, which only magnified my failures.

"Randy, what's wrong with you?" my mother often chided. "You are twenty-six years old and a hard worker. Why can't you get a job?"

"Your friends all have good jobs and are getting married and settling down," my stepdad would chime in. "What's your problem?"

I stood in the blackness of the night, alone on the bridge aside from the occasional car that whizzed by. It was too dark to see the water below, but I stared down at it anyway, imagining what it would feel like if I jumped. Would the fall kill me? Or would I drown in the icy waters?

One question kept replaying in my mind: What had I done wrong?

It's true I'd run with a rough crowd in high school and had gotten into a little trouble here and there, but I had completely cleaned up my act after graduation. I made new friends, turned my life over to God, and put myself through Bible College, determined to work in the ministry. But despite volunteering as an assistant chaplain at a nearby prison and chasing down every lead I came across, my dream profession as a pastor never materialized. The opportunities weren't there, and, beyond that, I realized I didn't have enough life experience to counsel others.

A few days later I was standing next to a pay phone, willing my hand to stop trembling as I placed a call to my friend, Barry.

I had managed to make it off the bridge that night without jumping—in part because I was scared of heights, but also because I realized I wouldn't solve anything by killing myself. But now I needed a place to stay. I had slept in my car the previous three nights but knew I couldn't keep going that way.

"Barry, listen, man," I started, hoping I didn't sound as desperate as I felt. "I'm kind of having a tough time right now and wondering if I might be able to sleep on your couch for a while. I could pay you $150 a month."

Barry lived in a basement suite he rented from his parents. I knew I was imposing on him and I hated asking for help, but I had nowhere else to turn.

The seconds seemed to stretch for hours as I waited for

Barry's reply. If his answer was "no," I was headed for another night in my car. And I wasn't sure how much longer I could handle that.

"Randy, you are about the only person I can think of that I could handle for a roommate," he said finally.

Conway's soft purring interrupted my time travel. I listened to the deep, steady rhythm of his purrs, wishing I could join him in his sleep.

Instead, I shifted my thoughts back to my to-do list, which suddenly seemed overwhelming.

1. **Go to the lottery commission to collect my money.** I hoped it wasn't a long-drawn-out process because I knew I wouldn't be able to relax until that money was in my bank account.

2. **Get out of town fast.** This meant finding someone I trusted who could immediately move into my house, watch over Conway, and become my assistant of sorts.

3. **Quit my job.** The irony was that when I had landed my position as an outdoor sales rep for Hertz Equipment Rental five years earlier, I had felt like I had hit the jackpot because my annual pay had doubled overnight. "It's like I've won the lottery," I had exclaimed to my mother at the time. Now, with a five and seven zeros floating around in my mind, that didn't seem like so much anymore, and I couldn't wait to walk away.

4. **Meet with church leaders** to obtain guidance and present them with a million-dollar check. I couldn't wait to see the look of joy on their faces when I gave them my tithing check. I knew how much this money would help—and I was thrilled to be of service.

I spent the rest of the night contemplating how to best execute my four immediate priorities. It was going to be a busy few days. But once I had my plan in place, I was going to be free to do whatever I wanted. I knew this meant having fun and doing some good. But with $50 million at my disposal, the opportunities for both were so wide open it was too much to process.

One thing I knew for certain: I had been gifted with this money and I was going to safeguard it. I knew what usually happened to lottery winners. The money turned into a curse; people lined up to take it from them—either by begging for it or stealing it outright—and within a few years it was gone. That was not going to happen to me.

3

A CROWD OF PEOPLE—INCLUDING AT LEAST a half-dozen TV and newspaper reporters—packed the foyer of the Alberta Gaming and Liquor Commission building in St. Albert, all waiting for me to make an appearance.

I could hear the buzz in my head as I listened for my cue. This wasn't a dream; it was really happening. In less than an hour, a wire transfer in the amount of $50 million was going to be deposited into my bank account. And in a minute or two from now, the world was going to know about it. It was so surreal my brain was having a hard time connecting to reality, in part because I knew that being handed $50 million in tax-free money didn't happen in real life.

"Are you nervous?" asked a staff member who'd coached me for the press conference.

Nervous wasn't the word for it. I had no problem speaking in front of large crowds—in fact I enjoyed it. But I was so jacked up on endorphins I couldn't stand still. I paced the room, trying to get a handle on it all. It had only been five days since that trip to the corner grocery store. But my life had already undergone a complete one-eighty.

It had started Sunday evening, when I knocked on Lisa's door unannounced.

Lisa was an apartment manager who had rented some equipment from me at Hertz, and we had developed a close friendship. I knew she was struggling financially. She was undergoing a nasty divorce after enduring an abusive marriage and was supporting both her mother and son. I also knew she was honest and hardworking and I had already been considering hiring her to clean my house and help with my expense claim ledgers. She was my obvious choice for the job I needed to fill.

"Lisa, I need you to come work for me. I've won the lottery," I blurted as soon as I walked through the door.

It was nearly ten p.m. and I could tell Lisa was tired and not in the mood for games.

"Yeah, I'd like to win the lottery, too," she smirked, taking a seat at her kitchen table.

Before I could say more, she picked up a document and handed it to me.

"Look at this, Randy," she said, pointing to the balance due line. "I thought I had already paid this off and they are telling me I still owe nearly $8,000. It's total crap."

I could feel her stress. I had been there before and knew what it was like to scrape pennies together, not knowing where the money would come from to cover the mounting bills. Now, with $50 million about to be delivered to my bank account, $8,000 was nothing.

"Lisa, don't worry about it. I'll cover it," I replied.

She looked at me like I had a few screws loose.

"I can take care of my own bills, Randy," she replied. "I'm just frustrated."

I could tell my message wasn't registering. I pulled out the lottery confirmation ticket from my pocket and pushed it in front of her.

"Lisa, I'm serious. I've won the lottery and I need to get out of town as soon as possible. I want to hire you to look after my house, handle my bills, and take care of Conway."

The amount I offered her, combined with what she was being paid to manage the apartment complex, doubled her salary. I could see her eyes widening as the reality sunk in.

I reached for my checkbook and wrote out a check for $25,000 to cover upcoming bills and her salary.

"This should get you started," I said as I wrapped up our conversation. "How soon can you move in?"

That had been four days ago and she was already settled into my house and developing a relationship with Conway—freeing me to embark on an indefinite, impromptu adventure.

The sound of the lottery commissioner's voice greeting the crowd gathered on the other side of the wall snapped me back to the present.

It was time.

Adrenaline shot through me as he made the announcement that signaled my entrance.

"It's my pleasure to introduce Alberta's newest multimillionaire!"

The audience roared with cheers as I ran through the streamer-filled archway, did a ta-da stance, and then made my way to the microphone.

I had rejected the idea of a press conference when the lottery commissioner first brought it up. Publicity was exactly what I was trying to avoid—it was the reason I was so keen on getting out of town. But when I expressed my concerns, he said going public would actually make life easier on me.

"What we've seen over the years is that if you do the press conference, the media will get their story and then leave you alone," he reasoned. "If you don't, they will continue to hound you."

I spent a few minutes mulling it over in my mind. I didn't want people knowing I was loaded because I didn't want them coming after me. At the same time, I had already hatched an escape plan. I planned to get a place near Vancouver, where, aside from my friends, I would be anonymous. On top of that, I planned to spend a lot of my time traveling over the next couple of years, meaning I wouldn't be around much to be recognized anyway.

The more I thought about the press conference, the more I warmed to the idea. I had just won $50 million. It was huge—the biggest thing that would ever happen to me. Why not turn it into a celebration and enjoy it with good friends?

I started making phone calls and arranging flights for Brent and my friends Ian and Hannah. They were now in the crowd cheering me on—along with Daryl, Ronnie, and a few other close local friends. We had all piled into the stretch limo sent by the lottery commission that morning and planned to continue the party after the press conference wrapped up.

The flash of cameras and lights snapped around me as I began answering questions. I told them how Conway Kitty had guilted me into heading out into the freezing weather and snow to buy the premium soft-serve cat food that led to my discovery that I had hit the jackpot. I also shared the story behind the numbers I had faithfully played for years. When they asked me what I did for a living, I explained that I "had" worked as an outdoor sales rep for Hertz Equipment Rental, which elicited a few chuckles.

"How long did it take you to decide to quit your job?" asked one of the reporters.

"About a nanosecond," I replied, causing the entire room to erupt in laughter.

With Lisa onboard to watch over my house and Conway, I had quickly moved on to the next item on my to-do list: Quit my job.

I had pulled up to my office at six a.m. Monday, hoping to get in and out before anyone else arrived. I backed my work truck up to my office door and began loading up personal belongings. I was nearly finished when Loren, a company mechanic who worked in the adjoining shop, spotted me.

"What are you doing?" he asked, eyeing the box I was carrying. "Are you quitting?"

I had a friendship with Loren and didn't want to lie. But I also wasn't ready to share the news so instead I skirted it.

"Actually, I'm retiring," I replied. "I had a few investments come in and I just decided to go for it."

Loren nodded and smiled.

"Good on you, man," he said. "I know you haven't been happy these past few months."

To say I wasn't happy was a serious understatement. I was miserable and had already been putting out feelers with other companies. It wasn't the job itself I disliked; it was the politics and games being played. The corporate bigwigs had started taking away our accounts and messing with our commission structure and I knew my paychecks would soon be taking a big hit.

I had intended to avoid other employees, but as I walked by the service counter on my way out, I saw the service manager reading the car section of the newspaper and couldn't resist. We were both big car nuts and were constantly checking what was out there.

"Are you buying a Lamborghini, Tony?" I asked, motioning to the luxury car section he was scanning.

"Yeah, I wish," he replied.

I put my arm around his shoulder and leaned in. "You know,

you'd almost have to win the lottery to afford a car like that."

It wasn't until later that morning—after I'd stopped by the lottery commission office and obtained an affidavit verifying my win—that I decided to call my supervisor and make it official.

Ray was taking the day off from work and I didn't like having to bother him at home. But I couldn't stand the thought of working another day and needed to get my resignation out of the way.

"Ray, if you could have any motorbike you wanted, what would it be?" I asked as soon as he answered his phone.

I could hear the surprise and confusion in his voice.

"Why are you asking?"

"Just go with it," I prodded.

"Well, I guess I would have to say a Harley Nightrider," he said after a few seconds of silence. "But I know you're not calling me up at home to ask me that."

He said it as a statement but I could hear the question in his voice. Ray wasn't one to play games and I knew he wanted to get to the point.

"You're right," I replied. "I want you to go pick it out for yourself. I'm buying.

"I'm retiring," I continued before he could say a word. "I've won the lottery."

Ray's reaction mirrored the reaction everyone else had.

"You're joking, right?"

Even though I'd had forty-eight hours to process the news, it was still hard for my mind to grasp. I was a welfare kid who had grown up on the wrong side of the tracks and had learned early on that if I wanted something, I had to fight tooth and nail for it. I hadn't been given anything in life, so to suddenly be handed $50 million was impossible to wrap my brain around. But even if I couldn't quite grasp the idea that I now had $50 million to my name, what I could comprehend was that I had plenty of money to do whatever I wanted—and to touch a lot of lives.

"Ray, would I phone you up on your day off and lie about something like this?" I asked.

I told him my resignation was effective immediately, but that I would be happy to wrap up any projects. Then our conversation returned to the Harley.

Ray didn't say anything for a minute. I knew he was having a hard time digesting it all. He and I had a love/hate relationship and had our share of disagreements during my five years at Hertz—especially in recent months, given all the negative changes afoot.

"That's really generous of you, Randy. But that's a lot of money. Why would you do this for me?"

I could feel the smile breaking open across my face. After all the negativity of the past few months, it was nice to be able to end our relationship on a high note.

"You gave me a job, and at the time it was a game changer," I said, a surge of gratitude moving through me as I recounted the memory. "My annual salary doubled and it was a huge jump in lifestyle. I want to thank you and this is my tip."

I hung up with Ray and started driving toward the Porsche dealership.

I wasn't a stranger there. I already had one Porsche and was constantly going to the car shows. But mostly it was just to drool over the latest models. Those days were over.

I walked into the sale rep's office and closed the door.

"How's it going, Randy? What can we do for you?" he asked.

I pulled out my affidavit from the lottery commission and pushed it across his desk. I watched the shock sweep across his face as he studied the document.

"You're kidding," he said finally, looking back up at me.

It was a response I was beginning to savor.

"It's for real," I replied. "Let's buy some cars, buddy."

❖

The reporters' questions were beginning to wrap up but there was still one big question.

"What are you going to do with the money?"

It was a question that had been swirling nonstop in my mind since leaving the corner grocery store on Saturday.

During my shopping spree at the Porsche dealership, I had splurged on two fully-loaded cars—including a beige 911 Carrera convertible with a cocoa-brown leather interior that I'd been salivating over for several months. Along with cars, I was passionate about travel and I couldn't wait to get out there and explore the world.

I knew I would invest some of the money in real estate and that I would make life easier for some of my close friends. But that still left a lot of money—and I knew I wanted to use it to do good.

I kept thinking about all the hungry, needy children in the world and all the people who were struggling to survive each day.

Though I'd always had a roof over my head and plenty to eat as a child, growing up on welfare wasn't easy and I understood what it was like to be without. And it only took thinking back on that life or death moment on the bridge all those years ago to feel the pain and despair that came with not having any money or even a place to stay.

The weight of the enormous responsibility I'd been given bore down on me as I tried to verbalize my thoughts and intentions.

"When I was twenty-six years old, I was close to being

homeless and I've never forgotten the experience," I started out.

The mood in the room had shifted from light to somber, and everyone had gone quiet.

"To whom much is given, much is expected," I continued. "This is a gift from God and it's a responsibility. I'm going to set up a trust fund, and the interest that spins off from it will go to feed hungry kids and homeless children around the world.

"A lot of people have nothing and I have so much," I added. "I want this money to do a lot of good, even after I am gone."

4

I DECIDED TO KICK OFF MY new life by giving away a million dollars.

It was a figure I'd settled on a couple of days earlier and I had spent several hours thinking through the list of people I wanted to help. I had come up with approximately twenty names and had scribbled down a number next to each. In most cases, I just picked an amount I wanted to give. But when it came to my closest friends, I focused on their individual needs.

"Make out a list of all your debts," I'd said to each of them. "This isn't a handout, it's a hand up and it's a one-time gift only. But I want to do this to help you out."

It was an amazing feeling to be in a position to make life easier for loved ones and strangers alike, and I'd been having fun surprising people.

Some were small gifts, such as the $100 tip I'd left for the waitress who had served me and my friends breakfast at Denny's that morning. Others were larger, like the SUV I gave to a woman I'd worked with at Hertz because she'd expressed a need for one the week before my win.

The biggest surprise I had delivered so far was for my friend Dave Crawford, whom I loved like the beloved uncle I always wished I had.

I'd met him at church three years earlier and we had immediately hit it off. Dave, who was nearing his fifty-ninth birthday, was a simple, down-to-earth guy. He was pudgy, dressed a little frumpy, and was a bit awkward. But he was one of the warmest people I had ever encountered. There was something endearing about him—right down to his trademark handlebar mustache. We had shared a lot of our personal struggles with each other and I knew he had endured a lot of hardship. Eight years earlier, he'd been in a motorcycle accident that left him out of work for a while and it had taken a toll on his finances. I knew he and his wife, Shirley, rented their home and had little to fall back on for retirement. And now that money was no issue for me, I couldn't wait to help relieve their financial stress.

I showed up at Dave's house unannounced on Sunday afternoon, shortly after church service. I had scanned the pews looking for him, but he wasn't in attendance and I was so amped up over the surprise I had in mind for him that I was about to burst.

I pulled up to his home in Sherwood Park, an Edmonton suburb, and knocked on his door.

"Well, hello, brother," he greeted me. "It's great to see you. How are you doing? Would you like to come in for some coffee?"

I could feel the joy surging through me as I followed him into his living room. I knew I was about to change his life and the thought was so exhilarating it was hard to hold it in.

"Sorry to bug you," I said as I took a seat on his sofa, hoping my tone didn't give it away. "I just want to take a few minutes of your time."

We usually met up at church so it was out of the norm for me to show up at his house. But Dave didn't seem fazed.

"Well, of course, brother," he replied as he put on a pot of coffee.

I waited patiently while the coffee brewed, making small talk until he had brought in our mugs and settled into his seat across from me. I took a couple of long sips of coffee. Then I reached into my coat pocket and pulled out the lottery ticket receipt, which hadn't left my sight since my trip to the corner grocery store the day before.

"Listen, something happened yesterday that I want to tell you about," I said. "For now, though, I just need you to keep it between us."

Dave looked at me curiously. "Of course, brother, what is it?"

I laid my ticket on the coffee table in front of him and let it rest there in silence for a few seconds while I took another sip of coffee. Then I spoke the words that were still so unbelievable my brain couldn't fully register them.

"I've won the lottery. Fifty million dollars."

For a few seconds Dave didn't speak. He just stared at the ticket receipt. I could see his facial expression shift from shock to excitement.

"Well, this is really wonderful," he finally said. "Does this change our friendship?"

His response caught me off guard. Why would it affect our friendship? My friendship with Dave was nearly all I had thought about over the past twelve hours. I was so revved up by my lottery win that it had been impossible for me to fall asleep. After reviewing my mental to-do list at least a dozen times and mapping out a detailed execution strategy for each item, my thoughts had switched to Dave. I had spent the early morning hours thinking through ways I could help him long-term—something that could be considered a win-win for both of us. I knew from past conversations that it was hard for him and Shirley to cover their monthly rent. I also knew that I wanted to invest some of my winnings in real estate. And that's when it hit me. I could feel Dave's eyes on me, waiting for my response. This was the moment I had been envisioning all night.

"Of course it doesn't affect our friendship," I started, looking at him intently. "Listen, Dave, what I want to do is buy a house and let you and Shirley live in it. And I'll pay you $2,500 a month to watch over it. Just give me a few months to get everything sorted out."

The room went silent. I watched my words register on Dave's face. It was like seeing a mood ring change color. At first, he had no expression at all. It was like he was too stunned to absorb what I was saying. I watched him shake his head, as though he was trying to clear his mind. Then I saw his eyes light up and his handlebar mustache shift as he smiled.

When he spoke, his voice contained so much joy and gratitude I could feel it in my core "Thank you so much for this, brother. This means everything. Thank you!"

❖

The lottery commission had delivered my friends and me back to the Porsche dealership, where we had all met and been picked up that morning for the press conference. A few of them had to get back to work, but Brent, Ronnie, Ian, Hannah, and I piled into the two Porsches I had just purchased. The plan was simple: Go to the bank to get the certified checks containing my money gifts issued, check into a hotel, and start celebrating

As we drove toward TD Bank, I thought about the first million I had tried to give away several days earlier. I was committed to my faith and had planned to cross off the next item on the to-do list I'd composed in my mind: Issue a check for a million dollars to my church.

On the advice of Pastor Craig, I'd shown up at the Monday morning staff meeting held by all the church pastors and elders. I couldn't wait to share my news, seek guidance on how best to proceed, and present them with the money. But when I explained that something big had happened to me over the weekend and showed them the lottery ticket receipt, they acted like I had robbed a bank.

"What have you done, Randy?" Pastor Gordon started, his tone scolding. "Don't you know that's gambling? You already have a good job. Did you want to be rich or something?"

His response was so unexpected that for a moment I couldn't speak. I'd come to them for advice on how to best utilize the money to do good, and had been so excited to present them with the million-dollar check that I'd had a hard time sleeping the previous night. I had expected them to be happy for me and thrilled to help me put the money to good use. Why was he treating me like I'd just committed a crime?

I could feel my neck hairs stand on end as his words continued to sink in.

Of course I wanted to be rich. It gave me freedom and meant I could retire, travel the world, and do good. Who wouldn't want that? And what was wrong with playing the lottery?

I locked my eyes on Pastor Gordon. Even without his six foot four frame, he had a towering presence that commanded everyone's attention. I concentrated on keeping my voice steady and calm.

"I really don't see it as gambling," I said. "I only spent a few dollars each week, and my mortgage and bills were always paid."

Pastor Gordon shook his head.

"Playing the lottery is definitely gambling," he reiterated.

Now I was really getting worked up. I didn't view playing the lottery as gambling.

But even if it was gambling by his definition, what did it have to do with my faith?

"Where in the Bible does it say gambling is bad?" I challenged. "The only time gambling is mentioned at all is when Jesus was being crucified and Roman soldiers gambled over his cloak."

It was clear that theological battle lines were being drawn, but none of the other church leaders were taking a stand. They all just looked to Pastor Gordon for a response.

"You're right," he said finally. "The Bible doesn't forbid gambling and it doesn't encourage gambling. It just doesn't talk about it."

I looked up to Pastor Gordon and the other church leaders. The last thing I wanted was for this to devolve into a screaming match. I took a deep breath to calm myself, hoping I could somehow salvage this meeting and get back to the reason I'd come.

I once again locked my eyes on Pastor Gordon. "You know I feel strongly about tithing. I had planned to give you a check for a million dollars."

If he wanted to change course, he didn't show it.

"Well, we can't accept it," he said. "We can't accept proceeds from gambling. It's against Church bylaws."

I certainly didn't want to give a million dollars to a person or entity that didn't want it. But his response still stung—both because I knew how much the money could help the church and congregation, and because, from my viewpoint, his line of reasoning was ridiculous.

"How do you know where that money is coming from when you pass around the plate on Sundays?" I asked, scanning the room as I spoke. "And what's the difference between buying lottery tickets and buying stocks, or buying a piece of land on speculation and then selling it five years later?"

Pastor Gordon didn't speak for a minute, but I could hear him thinking.

"We can't take proceeds that are a result of gambling—it's in our bylaws," he said finally. "However, we can accept the interest that accrues from it."

I respected Pastor Gordon and knew he was acting in accordance with Church rules. But I had left that meeting with a pit in my stomach. I'd tried to do something good with the enormous financial gift I had been given, and somehow my good intentions had turned into something bad.

❖

Steve, the VP of Operations at the bank, was waiting for my friends and me when we arrived—ready to personally assist with the bank drafts. It was amazing what a $50- million deposit could get you in terms of personalized service from bank bigwigs. Steve greeted us warmly and ushered us into his office, where he began the process of issuing certified checks that matched the names and amounts on my list.

The last person on my list was my mother. Given our estrangement, I hadn't told her about my lottery win and, as far as I knew, she wasn't yet even aware that I was now loaded. But I knew that would change soon and I wanted to have something ready for her.

It was surreal to be in a position to write my mother a $100,000 check and know that I could provide her with anything she needed or wanted. It was as though the family wealth that she had always felt should have been hers had finally come full circle.

"You know your grandma came from serious money," my mother would say as she divvied out her small welfare checks to cover our rent, pay our bills and make sure I had everything I needed. "Her grandfather hit it big in oil and was extremely wealthy.

"My mom's mother went to fancy private schools and was chauffeured around in limousines," she would continue. "But my mom was the black sheep of the family. Her parents were staunch Catholics and when she married an atheist, her family disowned her."

Though I loved my mom, we had a difficult and painful relationship. She was judgmental and controlling, maybe because her childhood had been so out of control.

My mom spent the first two years of her life in foster care because her mother was a raging alcoholic and didn't feel equipped to care for both her and my Aunt Amy, who was only eighteen months older.

Though my grandfather eventually brought my mom home, she never overcame the ingrained emotional pain the abandonment caused. And her emotional trauma only intensified when my grandparents divorced when she was eleven or twelve. My grandmother continued to be such a severe alcoholic that my mom essentially raised herself. Then she became pregnant, gave birth to me at seventeen, and dropped out of high school to care for me.

Despite our clashes, there was no question that my mother had done everything she could for me while I was growing up. She had raised me without a penny of support from my biological dad, and though we were on welfare for the first eleven years of my life, no one would have guessed it. She always kept our apartment spotless, made sure I had decent clothes to wear, and always had plenty of food on the table.

She had also instilled in me a strong work ethic, good

manners, and an unwavering understanding of right and wrong.

Steve finished processing the certified check for my mother, making all of the bank drafts complete. But I had one final piece of business I needed to work out with him. It had to do with my lottery win deposit.

I had a phone app that signaled me when the money had been deposited into my account. But instead of saying $50 million, it showed a deposit amount of $49,999,986.

"Steve, listen, I don't mean to complain, but I just had $50 million deposited in your bank and you charged me a $14 wire transfer fee. Really?"

I could see the color drain from his face. I couldn't imagine too many customers made $50 million deposits at the bank, and I knew what it would mean if I decided to pull my money.

"Oh, I'm so sorry, Randy," Steve muttered. "I don't know what happened there. I'll get that reversed right away."

❖

With the money gifts out of the way, I had only one thought on my mind: celebration time.

"Where should we go?" I shouted as the five of us piled back into the two Porsches. "Let's do this right."

I was on such an endorphin high that it was like I was floating outside of my body, watching the events unfold. Only a week earlier, I'd been making the rounds to my customers in my work truck—trying to force a smile on my face while mentally scrambling to figure out where I could land another job before pending corporate changes cut my salary in half. Now I had more money than I could envision spending.

Even though my money was currently sitting in a bank account and was earning only three percent, that still amounted to $1.5 million a year in interest alone—which broke down to nearly $4,000 a day. The interest was roughly seven times the salary I had been making. And with that kind of money, I reasoned I could afford to splurge.

It didn't take us long to settle on the Fairmont Hotel Macdonald, the most lavish hotel in Edmonton. It was where all of the celebrities and world dignitaries—including Queen Elizabeth II—stayed when they were in Edmonton.

We parked, grabbed our suitcases, and headed to the check-in counter.

"We need a suite that can accommodate all of us," I announced to the hotel clerk. "Do you have anything available?"

"Absolutely," she replied. "Do you have something particular in mind?"

As a matter of fact, I did. "Where did Paul McCartney stay when he was here?" I'd been a huge Beatles fan ever since hearing the song "Baby You Can Drive My Car" on the radio and discovering the *Rubber Soul* album as a teenager. I especially idolized Paul McCartney. I was such a huge fan that I had joined other groupies at the Fairmont Macdonald when the legendary musician was in town the year before, hoping to encounter him and convince him to sign my ukulele. I knew Paul McCartney loved ukuleles and I had retrieved mine from home, thinking it might grab his attention.

Though I'd failed to get the signature—which his bodyguard explained wouldn't happen because fans had started selling signed memorabilia on eBay—he had walked right past me before climbing into an Escalade and rolling down his window.

"Hey, Paul," I'd yelled, holding up my instrument.

He smiled, pointed to my ukulele, and shouted, "Aye"— which had been almost as good as his autograph.

"He stayed in the Queen's Suite," the desk clerk replied, interrupting my thoughts.

I knew the Queen's Suite was the most expensive suite in the hotel. But I didn't blink.

"Okay, let's take it," I replied, handing over my credit card.

I felt like a rock star myself as I headed to the top floor of the hotel with my friends. Out of curiosity, I'd asked how much the suite cost. The hotel clerk told us that in high season, the suite went for $6,000 a night. But because it was a Thursday night in early February, she gave it to me for $1,800—which my money was now earning every twelve hours or so.

I unlocked the door and walked into a suite that was so classically beautiful it looked like it belonged in Buckingham Palace. The suite was as big as a house, 2,400 square feet in all. We entered a lavish dining and living room area that contained twenty-one-foot-high ceilings and sweeping views of the city. Two separate wings led to suites to accommodate my friends, and a winding staircase took me to the master suite, where I was staying. Photographs of previous royal visits lined the staircase. The suite included a large balcony where, according to the hotel, Carol Burnett once sang the song "Don't Cry for Me Argentina."

"You've got to come check this out!" I called down to my friends.

We all stood on the balcony in the freezing winter temperatures, taking in the magic of our surroundings.

My high was so intense I felt like a rocket launching from the Kennedy Space Center. This was where all the top celebrities stayed—people like Bill Clinton and Mick Jagger. And now it was my world too. I pulled out the bottle of single malt scotch I'd picked up at a liquor store that specialized in bourbon and headed down to the main living area to kick off a celebration toast.

"Not a bad way to live," I said as I lifted my glass.

We spent the next few hours sipping bourbon, enjoying

conversation, and taking in our stunning surroundings. We dined at the hotel restaurant and then headed back to the suite to savor the experience.

I didn't sleep much that night. I just lay in the bed where the Queen had lain and thought about my life. The only plan I'd made so far was to head from here to Vancouver with Brent, who had taken a couple of weeks off from work. From there, maybe we'd go to Vegas or Hawaii. Or wherever we felt like going.

The voice just kept replaying in my head: You don't have to worry about money or work anymore. You are free to do anything you want to do. ANYTHING.

I headed to the bathroom, which was as big as a studio apartment. It featured a double Jacuzzi soaking tub, a walk-in shower, and bidet. But there was only one thought running through my mind as I sat on the toilet: Paul McCartney sat here.

We had been so busy celebrating that I had forgotten to check the nightly news for my press conference. But by the time morning rolled around, I was curious. My friends and I gathered around the large TV screen in the living room and flipped the channel to the CBC news station. Within a few minutes a news clip of my press conference appeared on the TV screen with national news anchor Peter Mansbridge sharing my story.

The headline read: Conway Kitty and Alberta Owner Win Millions. We all burst out laughing.

"You can't make this stuff up," I howled. "Maybe I'll get Conway an agent." After collecting ourselves, we logged onto the Internet to check out the other news stories about my lottery win. In nearly every case, the headline focused on Conway.

My fiery, twenty-seven-pound Maine Coon cat was a national celebrity.

5

BY THE TIME I CHECKED into the Ocean Promenade Hotel on the British Columbia coast in late February, I was so exhausted I could hardly function.

In my years of visualizing my lottery win, I'd never considered the toll an ongoing rocket ride through space took on a person's body. I was so charged up that I couldn't sleep. I was buzzing as though I'd downed a dozen espresso shots, and between my lack of sleep, continual adrenalin rush, and nonstop celebrating, I was a wreck.

After checking out of the Hotel MacDonald, Brent and I had flown to Vancouver for a few days to reconnect with old friends. From there, we had headed to Vegas to continue the celebration. I had invited a couple of other friends to join us and had even brought Brent's mother along. Marilyn had been like an aunt to me while I was growing up and I wanted to do something special for her.

"Who brings their friend's mom to Vegas with them to party?" Brent had protested when I raised the idea.

Since I was footing the bill, I figured it was my choice.

"I do," I replied firmly. Like in Edmonton, I had splurged on a lavish suite for all of us, choosing the one in Caesars Palace where the movie Rain Man had been filmed. We had lived it up, enjoying expensive dinners and indulging in shopping sprees for designer clothes.

My celebration had been fun. But I felt guilty and even a little disgusted by my excess spending and was now ready to buckle down and get serious about my future. I had offered to take Brent and his family to Hawaii in mid-April, but, aside from that, I had no plans and was determined to keep it that way.

I needed some time to rest, think, process everything that had happened to me, and develop a game plan for my new life. More than anything, I needed solitude.

My room had a balcony overlooking the rocky Pacific coastline, and I spent hours just staring out at the water, breathing in the salty air as I listened to the waves crash.

That's what I was doing when the phone call came. Without thinking, I answered it.

"Hey, Randy, it's Jeremy Crawford," said the voice on the other end. "My dad gave me your number and told me he didn't think you'd mind if I called."

I wasn't in the mood for conversation, and had it been anyone else, I would have hung up the phone. But since this was Dave's son, I made an exception.

"No problem at all, Jeremy," I replied, forcing my voice to sound cordial. "What's going on?"

In some ways, I felt like I knew Jeremy because Dave talked about him constantly. He lived in Arizona but I had met him briefly at church a few months earlier when he was staying with his dad. I'd actually donated several hundred dollars to him via Dave on two separate occasions because Dave had told me

Jeremy's wife was ill and they were struggling to make ends meet.

Jeremy didn't waste any time getting to the reason for his call.

"Everything's great with me," he said. "But listen, Randy, I've been working on this software project for three years now and I would love to show it to you."

My internal guard immediately kicked in. In the three weeks since my win, I'd already been approached by several people wanting me to invest in their business ventures. I knew this happened to lottery winners and had already prepared for it when compiling my mental "What to Do When I Win the Lottery" checklist.

"Listen, Jeremy, I'm not investing in anything for at least a year," I replied, repeating the words I'd said to the others who had hit me up for money. "I just want to let things settle down and figure out what I want to do with my life."

Jeremy was quiet for a minute.

"I understand," he said finally, "but would you just want to have a look at it?"

I could feel my gut tighten. I knew I wasn't going to invest and just wanted some alone time. But I also didn't want Dave to think I was being rude to his son. So out of respect for my friend, I once again made an exception.

"I guess it doesn't hurt to take a look," I said. "As I told you, I have no plans to invest in anything right now. But if you want to come down, I'll get you a room and you can show me what you have."

Three days later Jeremy was in my hotel suite, flipping through a PowerPoint presentation on KULTiD (Kult I.D.), his software program.

Though I had only agreed to meet him as a courtesy to his dad, there was something magnetic about him, and I could feel myself being pulled in. Jeremy had a strong, charismatic personality, and though I knew that he had struggled financially in the past, he radiated success. Like his dad, Jeremy stood about five foot nine and had a stocky, heavyset build. But unlike Dave, Jeremy dressed in expensive clothes, had a polished preppy look, and wore thick, black-rimmed glasses that exuded power and intelligence.

"I'm telling you, Randy—this is the next Facebook," he said as he began walking me through the software. "We've already got a lot of investors interested because they want to get a piece of it."

After a high-level overview of his KULTiD software concept, Jeremy had offered to take me through his more in-depth investor presentation if I signed a Non-Disclosure Agreement.

I had been intrigued enough to go along and was now definitely glad I had.

There was something intoxicating about the power of technology to transcend physical boundaries, connect people globally, and provide anyone, anywhere, with access to the information, goods, and services they wanted or needed. And as Jeremy continued flipping through the PowerPoint deck and talking through the functionality of the software he was developing, I could feel myself getting excited. What he presented was a touch-and-tag software that enabled consumers to see an image of a product—say, a pair of shoes—on their phone screen, touch it, and immediately learn the price and product details. The consumer could click on the item to purchase it immediately. Jeremy explained that as a wholesaler, KULTiD received ten percent of each sale. But that was just the starting point.

"The real power of the software is its social media/customer loyalty component," Jeremy explained. "As soon as the purchase is made, the software spiders through all of the consumer's social media accounts, notifying everyone that he or she is connected to about the purchase with the same touch-and-tag functionality. When anyone in the consumer's social media network makes a purchase, half of the ten percent sales revenue KULTiD receives goes back to the consumer in the form of KULTiD credit that can be used to purchase other merchandise."

My endorphins were once again kicking in. This had some serious legs, because each time a purchase was made, it was advertised through yet another entire social media network. It was brilliant.

"Check out these numbers," Jeremy said as he went through the sales projections. The exponential growth was staggering—into the billions.

"This is really cool," I admitted as he wrapped up his presentation. "I can definitely see how this could take off."

Jeremy took my enthusiasm as his opening.

"So many investors are lining up and things are moving fast. I just need $5 million more."

I didn't even know where to begin with that pitch. He threw out the words "five million dollars" as casually as if he were asking for a glass of water. I wasn't sure what world he was living in, but it was clearly not mine.

"No," I said flatly. "I don't care whose son you are. That's a lot of money and I don't work that way."

Jeremy reacted like I had just slapped him across the face. His mouth dropped open and his cheeks flushed. He looked so upset and deflated it almost made me feel bad.

I didn't mean to insult him, because he had definitely gotten my attention with his software concept and I knew I wanted to know more. But there was an ocean to cross before I was ever going to part ways with $5 million.

"Look, I love what you presented, but I don't know much

about technology," I said, trying to soften the blow. "I have a friend, Trevor, in Edmonton, who is a real techie. I'd like him to take a look at it. But keep in mind, this is a process and it's going to take time."

❖

I spent the next week savoring my new life. Being back on the BC coast after more than fifteen years away was like a homecoming for me. I had moved to Calgary when I was thirty-one in pursuit of affordable housing and a better paying job in the printing press industry, where I had finally landed a job. But my heart had always belonged to the west coast. During the long brutal Alberta winters, I would fantasize about the moderate climate, the water, and the breathtaking scenery. I couldn't imagine anywhere I would rather live and I knew it was where I would go when I retired. I had it mapped out in my mind. I had chosen the age of sixty-two as my hard stop retirement date. By then, I knew I would have my house paid off and figured I could sell it for $400,000 to $500,000, giving me a decent nest egg. During those frigid winter daydreams, I pictured my sixty-two-year-old self renting a small apartment somewhere on the west coast. To make my money stretch, I envisioned myself getting a part-time job at Starbucks as a barista. I loved coffee and I loved interacting with people so it seemed like an ideal fit.

I felt like I was floating as I moved along the boardwalk that lined the ocean bay, taking in the stunning ocean view condos that I could now have my pick of. Sometimes I would stop at one of the cafés to settle in with a steaming cup of coffee and the satisfying knowledge that my life of retirement no longer included a part-time job at a coffee shop. I didn't know what my post-retirement life looked like yet. But that was the beauty of being forty-eight-years-old and having a pile of money in the bank. I didn't need to know. I could just breathe and enjoy life and let my future materialize—though I was starting to sense that Jeremy's KULTiD software would play a role.

As much as I had tried, I couldn't get KULTiD out of my mind. I was a junkie when it came to stories behind the rise of global high-tech empires such as Apple, Amazon, and Facebook—stories of guys who started out in their garages or dorm rooms armed with nothing but a visionary idea that could transform society and the determination to turn that idea into reality. After spending my entire career on the dying end of business sectors such as printing, I was hungry for a ground-floor opportunity with an innovative high-tech company. It's something I had fantasized about for years and now it was like Jeremy was dropping that opportunity into my lap.

After I met with Jeremy, I called Trevor, a marketing executive with extensive high-tech experience. Trevor agreed to help me kick the tires on KULTiD and, like me, he found the concept compelling.

"I think he's really got something," Trevor reported after meeting with Jeremy and going through the presentation. "I've got a lot of questions because I'm not sure what the go-to-market strategy is or how he plans to roll this out. But the concept is incredible."

Trevor's cautious thumbs-up triggered a flurry of phone calls between him, Jeremy, and me over the next few weeks as we tried to learn as much as possible about the strategy to bring brands on board and develop the public awareness necessary to make KULTiD a success once the software app launched.

Though I could feel my excitement building, I was determined to take it slow and stick with my initial plan not to invest in any business ventures for a year. But Jeremy pushed back, arguing that when it came to such an innovative software application, speed to market was key.

"If we don't get out there soon, someone else is going to beat us to it," he stressed. "We've got to move because we are running out of time."

The further the discussions went, the stronger the pull. KULTiD was like a shiny new soccer ball and the more it was dangled in front of me, the more I wanted to play with it.

Though the timing was a little fast for my comfort level, I knew I needed to diversify my money. Having $50 million in cash sitting in a bank account didn't seem financially prudent or even safe. I needed to spread it out, which is why I was interested in real estate. I also knew that I eventually wanted to invest in high-tech, and, given all the synchronicities, it felt like my coming together with Jeremy was meant to be. It was something Jeremy honed in on as well.

"This really is a blessing, Randy," he noted. "The fact that you are best friends with my dad and came into this money just as I'm finishing this app really is a sign from God."

As our discussions continued, Jeremy filled me in on the early days of KULTiD. He explained that he had been working on the software concept three years earlier but had needed to put it on hold because his wife, Amy, was battling lupus—which had sent them shuttling back and forth between Arizona and Edmonton for treatment. But he said the break had actually been beneficial because it had enabled him to think through the concept and work out any of the bugs.

"I've taken it as far as I can go with it and now I need to bring in developers," he explained as he continued to push for money. "I've got to get this going."

An internal battle was brewing inside of me. I knew I wanted to be a part of this in some way. At the same time, I hated being pressured for money and still wasn't sure of the go-to-market strategy. As our back-and-forth discussions continued, tension started to build and it all came to a head in a hotel bar in Maui.

I had envisioned spending the first part of April relaxing on the tropical island before heading to Honolulu to meet up with Brent and his family for the vacation I had promised them. But Jeremy had been so relentless with his pressure for funding that I had invited him and Trevor to meet me in Maui to have some serious face-to-face meetings so we could drill down on the go-to-market strategy. I had tried my best to be accommodating. When Jeremy said he couldn't afford the trip, I had offered to foot the bill for him and even let him talk me into paying for Amy to come along. I was strongly opposed but he insisted, using Amy's illness to tug at my emotions.

"It's always been her dream to go to Hawaii," he argued. "And I almost lost her to lupus. Please, Randy. She really needs this."

After three days of discussion, Trevor and I still didn't feel like we had adequate answers. But when he pushed Jeremy on it that last night, tempers flared.

"Are you in, or are you out?" Jeremy snapped. "We've been at this for two months and all you guys want to do is talk."

His temper ignited mine and I was ready to go to blows.

"In or out of what, Jeremy?" I barked back. "All you've shown us is a PowerPoint."

The confrontation ended with Trevor stepping in as a mediator—which led to my decision to put up $150,000 for the mobile phone app development. I wanted in, but not too deep. In the scheme of things I reasoned to myself that $150,000 wasn't a lot of money. But I knew that if I was going to invest any more, I needed to check things out on the ground.

"As soon as I finish my vacation with Brent and his family, I'm coming to Arizona," I announced after agreeing to the initial investment. "I want to see your office and I want to meet your team."

6

JEREMY MET ME AT THE airport in a sporty, two-door convertible Mercedes—the perfect car for Arizona's balmy early May weather. It had been nearly three weeks since our heated exchange in Hawaii and the bad blood was now behind us.

"How's it going, brother?" he said in a warm, welcoming tone as I tossed my bag in the trunk and climbed in. "Welcome to paradise."

I was on such an elevated high that I was soaring as we drove through the breathtaking Arizona desert.

We both buzzed with excitement as we talked about KULTiD and the progress being made. Jeremy already had programmers working on the app development and had started putting together his staff. And after numerous conversations and updates from him while I was enjoying my tropical vacation, I was convinced that funding the app was one of the best decisions I had ever made. Jeremy was a visionary on a mission, and his charisma and drive were infectious.

"Let's go to the office so you can check it out and meet my new CFO," he said, as though reading my thoughts. "You are going to love him."

The KULTiD office building Jeremy had leased was located in the heart of Scottsdale and I was immediately impressed with the space. It was a two-level, 3,000-square-foot, condo-style office that seemed befitting for a cutting-edge tech company.

That feeling only increased when I met Ross Richardson, the new CFO, and Jacob, the Western Regional Sales Manager. Both men were well-dressed, well-spoken, and exuded the professionalism I wanted to see in a management team.

Having spent several years in sales, I had a good sense for what constituted a quality sales professional, and Jacob had the interpersonal skills and confidence that I knew were necessary for success. But, true to Jeremy's prediction, I was especially taken with Ross. He was bald, stood six foot six and had a commanding, charismatic presence that filled the company conference room where we were all seated. Ross looked to be in his mid-forties but already had an impressive resume. He told me that after playing college basketball, he had spent his early career in banking before becoming a partner in a group of senior assisted-living facilities that had just sold for $77 million.

"I pocketed several million and had planned to take a break from the business world," he explained. "But then Jeremy came along."

Calm washed over me as I took in his words. Ross wasn't just some guy off the street. He was a seasoned executive who knew his stuff.

My admiration only grew as he continued to talk.

"I planned to spend two years relaxing and pursuing my other passion: the ministry," he said, noting that he was currently working as an associate pastor at Christ's Church of the Valley—a well-known church in the area. "That's where I met Jeremy."

Given my faith and my own one-time dream to pursue a life in the ministry, this resonated deeply with me. Ross wasn't just an experienced CFO. He was a committed Christian and a man of God.

"It took Jeremy a while to convince me to join him because I really wanted to take a break," Ross added. "But once he walked me through the software, I was hooked."

The energy in the room was electric and any reservations I had about the viability of KULTiD were gone. It was like I had been invited to join an exclusive club and I felt privileged to be given such an incredible ground-floor opportunity. It was clear Ross was the big boy in the room, and if someone of his caliber was fully on board and steering the ship, it seemed a given that KULTiD was headed for huge success.

Ross and Jeremy walked me through a more detailed PowerPoint on KULTiD that drilled down on software launch timelines and addressed the go-to-market plan from a high level. They also talked about KULT Labs—the parent company—and other innovative software solutions they were envisioning. Then the conversation turned to funding needs.

Ross brought so much credibility to the venture that I knew I was interested in going further. But I still wasn't ready to invest a large sum of money.

"Jeremy, this is great, but I want to meet the programmers," I said as we ended our meeting.

The software app was being developed by the Nerdery, an outsource app development company located across town.

Jeremy hesitated. "Investors don't meet the programmers."

It was the same push and pull we had been engaged in since our first meeting.

We both were strong-willed, but he had to know I wasn't going to budge on this. "Well, this investor does," I replied in a tone that made it clear it wasn't up for negotiation.

Jeremy shook his head and laughed. "Okay. I'll make it happen."

We wrapped up our day and headed to the house Jeremy was leasing in an affluent Scottsdale suburb. He had insisted I stay with his family during my visit and I appreciated his hospitality. But I wasn't prepared for the nearly 5,000 square-foot estate. The home was beautiful and lavish, featuring a sprawling open-floor plan with a high-end chef's kitchen that flowed into a huge sunken living room. The house, which Jeremy told me came completely furnished, was clearly made for entertaining. The sectional sofa alone seated at least fourteen people and the expansive hardwood dining room table looked like it could hold even more than that.

"Wow, this is quite a spread," I noted as I took it all in. It seemed a little over the top but I realized that it was an ideal setting for Jeremy to schmooze potential brand partners for KULTiD.

After giving me a tour of the house, which included a master bath the size of a studio apartment, Jeremy walked me out to the garage to show me his prize possession: a fully-loaded Nighthawk Harley Davidson. And next to the bike sat an Audi A7. I knew both were expensive, but I was particularly taken aback by the Harley, which I knew retailed for at least $20,000.

"Nice bike," I said, moving in closer to admire its beauty. Jeremy's face lit up.

"Yeah, I picked it up a few years ago. I love it."

It was hard to reconcile that this was the same Jeremy I had met in church in Edmonton only seven months earlier—who, at least according to Dave, was so down and out that I had donated preloaded gas and grocery cards to help him and Amy. Given the circumstances, it seemed like a non-essential toy like the Harley would have been the first thing to go. But

I quickly shut this thought out of my mind. I was just getting to know Jeremy, so who was I to judge? It was clear he enjoyed the finer things in life but it was also clear he knew how to make things happen. I knew ups and downs went with being an entrepreneur. And I was convinced that Jeremy was ready to shoot straight up with KULTiD. It was why someone of Ross Richardson's caliber had come on board. And though I didn't yet know the extent of the role I would play, I was grateful to Jeremy for allowing me to join his game.

The next day we headed to the Nerdery to meet with the programmers assigned to the KULTiD project. I had met programmers in the past and had always found them emotionless. But when I asked them for feedback on the KULTiD software, their faces lit up.

"There have been a few attempts at this kind of platform, but you guys have got it right," the lead programmer explained. "This really could be the next Facebook."

I could see the "I told you so" grin spreading across Jeremy's face.

"Well?" he said as soon as we were back in the car.

I was so excited I could taste it. But as much as I wanted to be a part of this, I still couldn't bring myself to invest the $2 million to $5 million Jeremy and Ross had told me was needed.

"I need time to digest this," I told Jeremy as he drove me to the airport. "I really like this but it's out of my realm of investment experience.

"Just leave it with me," I added. "I have to think on it."

I spent the next couple of weeks turning it over in my mind. Aside from funding the app, the only experience I had investing money was in real estate. I liked real estate because it was a hard asset and usually always grew in value over time. It was where I was comfortable.

I made another trip to Phoenix in mid-May to check out

the progress. The software development was coming along as planned and Jeremy told me that Jacob was beginning to secure meetings with large merchandise manufacturers. But the underlying issue was the same: If they were going to bring this software to market before someone else beat them to it, they needed funding.

As much as I wanted in, I still wasn't ready to part with a pile of cash. But as I thought about the expenses Jeremy had to cover in terms of office space and the high-end house he was leasing for his family, an idea hit me.

"I think I've got a solution for what can keep us all happy," I said to Jeremy as I wrapped up my visit. "I know these last couple of years have been a struggle for you financially with Amy being sick, and I want you to be focused on work. So, here's what I'm thinking.

"I will buy the house you are leasing in Scottsdale and the house that your parents are leasing in Sherwood Park so you and Amy have a place to stay when you are in Edmonton for her treatment. I will also buy the office building that's for sale next door so you can move the offices into it. This way you don't have to worry about paying a mortgage or the office lease."

I could sense Jeremy beginning to relax as he took in my words.

"Here's the deal," I continued. "These assets will go in my name and when the company reaches the cash-flow stage and is equivalent to my investment, I'll transfer the assets over to you in exchange for five percent of KULT Labs."

It was like a pressure valve had been released. I could see the relief wash over Jeremy's face.

"Wow, that's so huge. Thank you! To not have to worry about all of that helps so much."

All in all, I was proposing an investment of just over $2 million—which I knew took a huge financial load off of

Jeremy. At the same time, I was safeguarding my investment by purchasing hard assets, which made me feel good. If all went as planned, I would own five percent of a surging, cutting-edge high-tech company. And if it didn't, I was only out the $150,000 I'd invested to get the app developed.

7

Jeremy and I were in the middle of breakfast at an Edmonton café a week later when he pulled out a document from his bag and laid it on the table.

"I've written up the agreement we discussed," he said, pushing the piece of paper toward me.

Now that I had settled on an investment plan that seemed bulletproof from a risk perspective, I couldn't wait to move forward with KULT Labs. As Jeremy put it, it was a rocket ready to launch.

"Okay, let's take a look," I said, pushing aside my plate.

Jeremy began walking me through the line items in the contract. There was the house in Sherwood Park as we had agreed to, as well as the office building in Scottsdale. There was also the Scottsdale house Jeremy was currently leasing. But the price tag listed was $150,000 more than the property price.

"The house needs a swimming pool," he explained before I could ask. "It's Arizona and this is an upgrade that will add value to the property."

My gut clenched a little as I absorbed that piece of information. It's not what I had put on the table and it bothered me that Jeremy had just stuck it into his draft agreement without first running it by me. But I also knew he had a point. Arizona was blistering hot half of the year and having a swimming pool in a high-end house was a given. And since it was my house anyway, his argument made sense.

"Okay, I can live with that," I replied, moving on to the next line item.

That's when I discovered Jeremy's next surprise addition: an extra $168,000 to cover the purchase of a fully loaded Audi R8.

I knew that he was as big of a car nut as I was. We had bonded over car talk and he had salivated over my most recent purchase: a black Ferrari 458 Spider that I called Boris, named after The Who song "Boris the Spider."

I didn't blame him for wanting an Audi R8. But I wasn't in the mood to foot one for him, either. Beyond that, Jeremy already owned a beautiful two-door Mercedes that looked to be brand-new. It wasn't like he was hurting for a vehicle.

"No, Jeremy," I replied. "That wasn't part of our deal."

He must have expected my response because he was ready for me.

"Randy, I need this," he pushed. "I've been working on this software app for three years. It's my time."

I had to give it to him: The guy had balls. It was almost entertaining to watch him work. He was like a kid working over his parents for the new video game he was determined to have. He was relentless but also charismatic and convincing. He had a way of making it sound like he was entitled to the car.

"Jeremy, we haven't done anything yet," I argued. "Let's get this going and then you can buy the whole damn lot."

Jeremy eyed me intently and shook his head.

"Randy, please. It's my time now. We both know the

company is going to take off. It's my time. And I've already put down a deposit on the car."

He was like the Duracell Bunny. He never stopped.

I spent a few minutes mulling over Jeremy's request. He was clearly jumping the gun and I hated being pressured in this way. At the same time, I knew we were on the verge of something big and it was because of Jeremy that I had a seat at the table. He was a little odd and over the top. But he had a gift when it came to selling his ideas and I knew this was what would send KULTiD skyrocketing. And though $168,000 was a lot of money, it wasn't much considering the windfall I had been given.

"Okay—fine, Jeremy. I'll do it," I relented, "but like everything else, the car goes in my name."

We finished going through the draft agreement that Jeremy had written up. Along with the hard assets, it included the $150,000 I had already invested and a cash infusion of $350,000 Jeremy had convinced me to include so he had some operating capital. Aside from the surprise addition of the swimming pool and Audi R8, everything looked to be in order. All told, my investment came to just over $2.61 million (slightly over $2 million in US dollars).

Jeremy reached into his bag and pulled out a pen. "It's good to go," he said. "All you have to do is sign."

Forget the Duracell Bunny. He was Tony Robbins on steroids.

I got that he was anxious to get things done. But this wasn't a $50 loan. It was a $2.6 million investment and I wanted to make sure everything was buttoned up.

"I can't sign this," I said, pushing the pen back toward him. "This has got to go to my attorneys."

Jeremy shot me an exasperated look and I could see the veins tighten in his neck.

"We don't have time for that," he said, his voice rising as he spoke. "I have to get back to Arizona tomorrow."

I'd had enough back and forth with Jeremy by now to understand that he operated on a high-intensity, accelerated pace. He was used to pushing people and getting his way, and I could see the benefits of this when it came to building out a company. But I wasn't the company—I was the investor. What's more, it irked me that he had already been in town for several days with his family but had waited until he was leaving before springing this on me.

"I'm sorry, Jeremy, but I don't work this way," I replied, repeating the words I'd spoken on numerous occasions over the past three months. "If this was so urgent, why did you wait until the last minute before giving it to me?"

The guy didn't seem to have an off button and was ready with his comeback before I had even finished speaking.

"Why are you digging in your heels, Randy? We've been going at this for three months, and this is what we agreed to. What's the problem?"

I was getting flustered. I wasn't trying to be unreasonable. I just wanted to be cautious.

"I'm not digging in my heels," I shot back. "I'm just not comfortable with this. I'm not used to working this way."

Jeremy's voice shifted from agitated to reason. "Randy, come on, you know my dad."

The hard-charging salesman sitting across the table from me was so opposite of Dave that it was easy to forget that Jeremy was his son. But the reminder had an immediate calming effect.

Jeremy was right: I knew his dad. And I trusted him with my life.

My relationship with Dave was different from my other friends—in part because he was older and played more of a mentorship role, but also because of our shared spiritual beliefs and devotion to our faith.

I didn't start my life as a Christian. In fact, I was a rowdy seventeen-year-old punk with a penchant for LSD when I first met the missionaries who would ultimately lead me to God. George and Eleanor Twedale, New Zealanders whom I met through my stepdad's homing pigeon club, had spent years working in Ethiopia and had recently fled with only the clothes on their back. They had nothing when they landed in Canada. But the church community had rallied around them—acquiring a house for them and donating food, furniture, and money to help them get on their feet.

I was struck by the caring and compassion of the people who had come to their aid. It was so foreign from the delinquent lifestyle I was leading with my friends. I knew I wanted that for myself. I was also struck by the way Mrs. Twedale talked about Jesus as a person—as though she had a personal relationship with him.

I decided to do my own research to determine if—outside of the Bible—I could prove that Jesus had really existed.

I began reading secular history books and researching scholarly articles until I was convinced he had really lived.

That was the final tipping point for me. Though I was still living a rowdy life, I could see the end of the road for most of the guys I ran with. I knew they would either end up dead or behind bars, and I didn't want that for myself.

I made a clean break from them as soon as I graduated from high school, stopped using LSD, and began attending a local Christian church. By the time I was nineteen, I was so immersed in my new faith I decided to enroll in Bible college and pursue a career in the ministry.

Though I didn't end up a pastor, I sought out volunteer opportunities to give sermons or lead gospel discussions whenever possible. That's how Dave and I had connected. We forged a bond during the year I led the men's group at our church. We both loved theology and often engaged in deep discussions about how to incorporate God's teachings into our daily lives.

Dave was a no-nonsense, down-to-earth guy who came with a great sense of humor and plenty of talent. He was a good singer who loved performing gospel songs for our church congregation and had such a gift for nature photography that his pictures stood up against any *National Geographic* photo I had seen. But it was his listening ear and kind words that attracted me most.

During our long conversations, I had told Dave about my family history and the potent combination of alcoholism and abuse. My maternal grandparents were drunks who had made my mom's childhood hell, and they hadn't played much of a role in my life. And my relationship with my mom and stepdad was so dysfunctional that we often went years without talking. Dave could relate to the struggles I had with my parents because he had a strained relationship with his dad, and he soon became my closest confidante. Whenever I was having a rough day, Dave was there to hear me out and offer encouraging words. After years of feeling like a lone soul, I no longer felt isolated.

Thinking about Dave and my love for him diffused any frustration or concern I had over Jeremy's push to get the contract signed and in place. Dave was like family—the good kind I had always longed for—and, by extension, that made Jeremy family, too.

Despite our different business styles, I couldn't blame him for wanting to get things solidified so he could focus on the software app.

I spent a few minutes in silence, combing through the draft contract again. There wasn't much to it: just a list of line items with dollar amounts and a couple of paragraphs that outlined the terms. But it covered all the key points important to me—specifically that the titles for the hard assets would go under my name until the company was worth at least as much as my investment, at which time the assets would be transferred to the company in exchange for a five percent stake in both KULTiD and KULT Labs.

My head was telling me it was still a good idea to have my attorney do a final review. But my emotions won out.

"Okay, fine," I said, reaching for the pen.

The next morning Jeremy and I were sitting in the city law offices of Fort Saskatchewan, where Shirley worked, facilitating the real estate transaction for the Sherwood Park house.

This, too, was an emotions-based decision. I had protested the idea of using Shirley to facilitate the transaction, arguing that it was a huge conflict of interest and could cause her a lot of problems if our business dealings ever went south. But Jeremy once again pulled out the relationship card.

"Randy, why are you being such a hard-ass?" he pushed. "Come on, you know my mom and dad. Nothing's going to go wrong and it's a lot easier this way."

I wasn't thrilled about involving Shirley and Dave in my personal business dealings. But I relented because Jeremy and I were both catching a plane in a few hours and I knew he had a point: Working with Shirley would definitely help expedite the process. But before I signed the papers, I made sure she was clear about the conditions of our agreement.

"Listen, Shirley, our arrangement is that this title goes under my name. Are you clear on that?" I asked, explaining the terms under which the property would be transferred to the company.

"Yes, I understand," she replied.

That was all I needed. "Okay—how much do you need for closing?"

The total came to just over $378,000, which I agreed to

have wired immediately.

"That's great, but this has just been thrown on me and I'm really busy right now," Shirley said. "If you sign the papers, I can get this filled out and handled later."

I quickly scribbled my name on the stack of documents and arranged to have the money wired for the closing. Despite my initial reluctance to use Shirley, I had to admit that it was nice to have her handling all of the administrative work without my needing to worry about anything. It felt good to have someone on the inside looking out for me.

On Jeremy's suggestion, I also directed my bank to wire him the money for the two Arizona properties so he could handle those transactions on my behalf.

"Okay, I think we are good to go," I said as Jeremy and I left the law offices. "Let's get this software launched."

8

I MIGHT HAVE BEEN RETIRED, BUT my life was now going a million miles a minute.

I was soon back in the Vancouver area, closing on two houses—including the one that would soon be home for Dave and Shirley.

After stopping by Dave's place after my lottery win to share the news and tell him my idea to put him up in a house, we had both started looking at property. Dave had found several listings in Alberta that he sent my way. But I had something special in mind for him.

I had always fantasized about living in a log-cabin-style home. I love the smell of cedar and the beautiful architecture and wanted to find one in the BC countryside.

A good friend who had been helping me in my search found the property in a wooded, rural setting located within an hour's drive of Vancouver. The second I set foot in it, I knew it was the one. It sat next to a river on nearly an acre of land and was the most stunning log home I had ever seen. It was more like a lodge than a house, with a wraparound deck, a cozy gas fireplace, and a large, open floor plan with a cedar trunk log serving as the main support post. The best part was that it had both an upstairs and downstairs suite, making it perfect for me to visit—and for Dave to live in.

He and I had often talked about our mutual love of the BC coast. It had everything: the vibrant city of Vancouver, the ocean, the mountains, and a moderate climate year-round. I knew it's where he longed to be and I couldn't wait to surprise him with the news.

I told the realtor I wanted the property and then immediately dialed Dave's number.

"Listen, Dave," I started, feeling the joy surge through me as I spoke, "I know you have always wanted to move to the Vancouver area and I've found a beautiful log-cabin home with a full suite downstairs that would work perfect for you and Shirley. You can say no and I will completely understand. But I would love to have you live there if it works for you and, as discussed, I'll pay you $2,500 a month to look after it."

I knew this meant that Shirley would need to quit her assistant job at the real estate law firm in Edmonton. But I also knew that without a mortgage to pay and $2,500 a month coming in, the two of them would be covered financially.

I didn't have to see Dave to know that a smile had broken open across his face. I could hear the euphoria in his voice.

"We are in, brother," he said without missing a beat. "I can't believe this. Thank you so much, brother."

I wanted the house to be perfect for Dave and Shirley and had already lined up contractors to redo the downstairs kitchen before I moved them in at the end of June.

Dave knew about that surprise. But what he didn't know was that I had bequeathed that house to him in my will, along with a one-time $500,000 payout and a $65,000 annual stipend.

His days of struggle were over. I was going to make sure he was set.

❖

Life was so good I mentally checked in with myself several times a day just to make sure it was for real.

I woke up every morning with such a huge rush of endorphins that I felt like I was on an amphetamine high.

The knowledge that I had so much money that I could buy virtually anything I wanted was intoxicating. But I alternated between euphoria and panic. I was now the steward of tens of millions of dollars, and while I wanted to enjoy it, I also was terrified of losing it and falling victim to the lottery-winner curse.

It's why I had mainly focused my investments on real estate.

I now owned five houses in Canada: my original house in Edmonton, the Sherwood Park house that would be available for the Crawfords' use, a house I had purchased in Ottawa so that Brent and his family had a free place to live, the log-cabin home where Dave and Shirley would soon be living, and another house in the BC countryside that I offered up to other close friends. And these were on top of the office building and home I now owned in Arizona.

Like my log-cabin home, the house I purchased in Ottawa had a separate suite reserved for me whenever I wanted to stay there. But for my primary living space, I had settled on a one-bedroom, top-floor condo on the beach with sweeping views of the BC coast.

The place was magic for me. This was a beach I had frequented as a child. The views were breathtaking and it was one of my favorite spots in the world.

I spent hours sitting with a steaming cup of coffee in front of my expansive floor-to-ceiling window, taking in the ocean bay and crashing waves, while thinking about that welfare kid from New Westminster who had once walked the boardwalk below. It was both exhilarating and mind-boggling to be able to call this paradise home.

Sometimes I felt like I was suspended in air—watching my new life unfold below me. Other times I felt like I was shooting around space at such a rapid pace it was hard to catch my breath.

I no longer operated on any sort of timetable. I just did whatever entered my mind—whenever it entered it. Mostly it came down to feeding my two passions: travel and rare sports cars.

Since winning the lottery, I had vacationed in Hawaii and the Mexican Riviera and had taken several spur-of-the-moment trips throughout Canada and the US to check out rare cars I had found.

Along with my initial splurge on the two Porsches, I now owned a few Ferraris and a Boxster Spyder that I had found during my vacation in Hawaii.

I don't know where my passion for cars came from, but I'd been obsessed with them ever since I could remember. In fact, one of the only two memories I had of my biological dad revolved around his car.

I was only four years old at the time and was walking up a large hill toward our apartment with my mom. My dad, who had just been released from prison for hijacking a tractor trailer loaded with color TVs and explosives, pulled up next to us.

"Want a ride?" he asked, opening the car door for my mom and me.

I don't remember much about the brief conversation that ensued between him and my mom. But I remember everything about the car he was driving. It was a 1965 Buick Wildcat convertible. It was midnight black: black top, black exterior, and black interior. It had an eight-ball shifter and a tachometer, which I later learned was very rare.

I only met my dad once more a couple of years later, when my mom ran into him at a bar and brought him out to the car where I was waiting to say hello. Like the time before, my memory of our conversation was a blur. But a detailed image of his car was seared in my mind. Maybe it was my way of connecting with him. Whatever the reason for it, I had every inch of that car memorized and described it in detail to my dad's brother when I tracked him down twenty-seven years later.

"How can you possibly know all of that?" he'd exclaimed in disbelief. "He only had that car for four months and you were way too young to remember."

I knew it was bizarre, but when it came to rare, older sports cars, it was how my mind worked. I was a certified car nut. And with tens of millions of dollars earning interest in my bank account, it was impossible for me to hold back.

The good part—the part that I was able to justify to myself—was that the cars I was chasing down were collector's items that, like my real estate purchases, grew in value.

"You can have fun and make money at the same time," I reasoned to myself as I combed yet another rare car website. "It's called a passion job."

9

Attention to detail had never been my strong suit, and I was now going in so many different directions that I was having a hard time staying on top of everything. The only time I slowed down enough to think was during the road trips I occasionally took to bring the latest car I had purchased back to the Vancouver coast.

I was on such a road trip around the first of July when it hit me that I hadn't asked Shirley about the title for the Sherwood Park property.

I had moved her and Dave into the log-cabin house a week earlier, and since Shirley had just quit her job at the real estate law firm, I wanted to make sure everything was in order.

I soon had her on speakerphone. But when I asked her to send me the documents, she dropped a bombshell.

"I can't because they aren't in your name," she said. "They are in Jeremy and Amy's."

Her words were so unexpected that at first I couldn't process them. What did she mean the title wasn't in my name? That was the whole point of the transaction and I had discussed it in depth with her.

"What's going on here, Shirley?" I demanded. "You had very clear instructions."

Shirley paused before answering. "Jeremy said you changed your mind."

I was so stunned I was having a hard time digesting what she was saying.

"No, no, no!" I thundered into the phone. "That is not what we agreed to and I didn't change my mind. I told you what the agreement was and you told me that you were clear."

Shirley was almost indignant in her response.

"Don't shoot the messenger," she replied. "This is between the two of you."

I hung up with Shirley, pulled over to the side of the road, and whipped off a message to Jeremy.

"Dude, what's going on here? I just talked with Shirley and she said the Sherwood Park house is in your name. That wasn't our deal and I want it fixed!"

My insides were on fire but my brain was a fog. How could he pull this on me? This was our deal.

Jeremy responded as though nothing was wrong.

"You're overreacting," he replied. "We could transfer it back in your name if you want, but it would cost about $1,000, and I think it's a waste of time and money because everything is going so well with the company, it's a moot point."

I could hear buzzing in my head as I tried to make sense of his actions. How could he think this was okay? My thoughts jumped to the purchase of the Arizona house and office building—which Jeremy had offered to facilitate on my behalf. My heart pounded against my chest as I shot off another email, asking about the Arizona titles.

"Things work differently here in the US, Randy, when it

comes to titles," he replied. "Closings are handled differently. We couldn't have you on the title because you weren't there to sign on closing."

His words landed so fast and hard they knocked the air out of me. By the time I could breathe again, I had so much adrenaline pumping through me I was shaking. I dialed his number and started laying into him as soon as he answered the phone.

"That's total BS, Jeremy!" I yelled. "I've bought a lot of homes in my life and have only been present for two or three of them."

Panic bubbled inside of me as my thoughts locked on the trip I had taken to Arizona three weeks earlier. I was so pumped up that I couldn't stay away and had flown down for a day to check out the progress. Like before, the energy in the office was electric and so intense it was hard to keep my feet on the ground. The app development was in full swing, and the programmers were telling us it would be ready to go live mid-October. This, as Ross and Jeremy reiterated, meant we needed to be ready with a roll-out strategy and launch that could capitalize on the holiday season.

Jeremy told me that he had found a couple of great sales and marketing executives he wanted to hire, to speed up the process of bringing on brands and signing up users, so it would all be ready to go when the software launched. But he was facing the same issue: money.

"Randy, we need more operating capital to keep going," he had confided during a lunch meeting between him, Ross, and me. "It definitely helps to have the office space and my mortgage covered. But we need money for employees, office expenses, and advertising."

Though I was much more comfortable limiting my investment to hard assets that could serve as collateral, I knew he was right. He and Ross were building this company from the ground up, and if we wanted to get this to market, it was going to require funding. It had been hard to make the first jump. But now that I had a stake in the company, I was determined to have it succeed. And it was empowering to know that I had the ability to make that happen.

"How much do you need?" I had asked.

It was clear Jeremy had thought this through, because he didn't miss a beat.

"Two million dollars in tranches of $500,000 over the next four months starting now. If you could do this, we could increase your ownership stake to ten percent."

My mind had raced through the calculations. Ten percent of a company that had the potential to generate billions of dollars was a lot of money, and investing another $2 million to get there was a no-brainer. It was like trading pennies for dollars.

"No problem," I had replied. "Consider it done."

My thoughts jumped back to the present, which now seemed like an alternate universe. How could Jeremy jeopardize everything in this way? I had already sent the first $500,000 payment, but I could put a stop to the money flow at any time. And then he would be screwed.

Jeremy responded to my angry rant with patience and calm, like he was trying to reason with a misinformed child.

"Yes, but that's Canada," he said. "It's different here."

I wasn't familiar with US law, but this didn't smell right to me. At the same time, I was beginning to calm down a little because I realized it didn't really matter what names appeared on the property titles. I had a contract spelling out the terms of our agreement. And that gave me all the protection and ammunition I needed.

"Do you realize what position you've just put yourself in, Jeremy?" I said, punctuating the words for emphasis. "This is contractual fraud."

If Jeremy was concerned by my reaction, he didn't show it.

"Randy, calm down. You are overreacting," he repeated. "It's all a moot point anyway because the company valuation is going through the roof."

My heart and head were once again in a standoff. What Jeremy had just pulled was fraud and inexcusable—or at least that's how it felt. But if he was telling the truth about real estate laws in Arizona, maybe he was right. Maybe I was overreacting.

I knew the software was coming along and that momentum was building. Jeremy had hired the two sales and marketing executives he had told me about and had even brought on a couple of lead programmers from the Nerdery in-house so they could concentrate on the KULTiD software as well as other cutting-edge software apps Jeremy was working on. The official company kickoff summit was happening the third week in July, and we had already talked about a massive product launch party at the end of October, with both media and celebrities in attendance to generate awareness and catapult KULTiD to instant success.

My brain was telling me that this was not right. But my emotions were in turmoil. We were so close to getting this app into the marketplace and maybe he was right, maybe it was all a moot point and I was getting worked up over nothing.

On top of that, I couldn't see Dave letting his son pull one over on me given that he and Shirley were now living in my house and I was essentially funding their retirement.

My hands were no longer shaking and I could feel the tension leaving my body. I was willing to give Jeremy the benefit of the doubt and let this one slide. But the internal guard that had kicked in when I first met Jeremy was now back on a twenty-four-hour watch. One thing was certain: I was done with these kinds of shenanigans.

"Jeremy, I don't do business this way," I stressed before ending the call. "This is not how I conduct my affairs. Either we do it the right way, or not at all."

10

I was living out of my suitcase, bouncing from one end of the continent to the other. When I wasn't traveling to destinations such as Florida or Toronto to check out a rare sports car, I was hopping down to Arizona to check in on KULTiD. And when I wasn't car hunting or monitoring the progress of Jeremy's mobile phone app, I filled my time with spontaneous leisure trips, such as the one I took to Vegas in July to catch the rock band Rush in concert.

The amphetamine high that kicked in the second my brain registered my lottery win was still pushing me forward in impulsive, sometimes uncontrollable bursts.

But I was also beginning to feel a void in my gut.

Lisa had brought Conway Kitty to the log-cabin house as soon as Dave and Shirley moved in so I could have easier access to him, and by mid-August I was in serious need of some Conway love.

My cats had always been a huge part of my family. Cats didn't come with the emotional baggage and control issues that wreaked so much havoc with human relationships. They just brought unconditional love and loyalty.

Just seeing Conway made me feel like I was home. He greeted me by brushing up against my legs and then jumping up on the couch next to me so I could run my hands through his fur.

"Like your new digs, Conway?" I asked, massaging his back like I always used to do. "I've missed you."

Being with Conway grounded me. He was a reminder of my pre-lottery-win life, when it was just him and me every evening and weekend. Conway always stayed within eyesight of me during the day, continually brushing up against my legs so I could feel his presence. But what I relished most was nighttime, when he would curl up in his familiar resting place next to my head. I was craving connection and the soul-nurturing love that pets provided. It was the kind of love I had experienced in spades with Conway's predecessor, Huey.

Just thinking about Huey made my heart hurt. He was a matted, scabbed-over mess when I first laid eyes on him at the SPCA in Calgary. They told me he had been found half-dead in the street and was so battered and malnourished they had planned to put him down. But on a whim, they had given him some medication and he had responded enough that they decided to put him up for adoption.

"There is something special about this one," the volunteer at the SPCA noted when she saw me eyeing him. "He's got some serious will."

I had gone to the animal shelter in search of a kitten. But the minute I saw Huey, I knew we were meant to be together. He was meowing angrily, clearly pissed off that he was locked inside a cage, and I connected with him instantly.

We were both scrappy and tough, had both survived the street, and were both starved for love. And we quickly became a family.

Huey—a tabby my vet guessed was around ten years old—was the most affectionate, caring cat I had ever encountered. While Conway always wanted to be near me, Huey always needed to be on top of me. When he wasn't curled up on my lap, he was pawing me on each shoulder—giving me his best version of a hug while licking my earlobes.

Everyone who met Huey fell in love with him. There was so much soul and depth to him. Maybe it was because he had gone through so much himself that he understood that all that really mattered was love, and he showered me with it.

I don't know how many lives Huey had gone through before we found each other. But it was clear it was his will to survive that kept him going.

The first time he should have died during our time together happened a couple of years after I brought him home. It was the middle of a brutal Alberta winter and a blizzard had hit the city. The snow was coming down so fast and hard that nearly two feet had accumulated since I had arrived at work, and we were sent home early to avoid accidents.

I fought my way through the blinding gusts of snow to my house, anxious to escape the freezing flurry of ice and wind and warm up with a cup of coffee and Huey. But when I finally arrived, my cat was nowhere to be found.

Panic shot through me as I searched each room, calling his name. It wasn't like Huey to hide and I knew this meant only one thing: He must have slipped outside when I left for work.

I ripped open my front door and headed back out into the storm.

"Huey!" I shouted as loud as I could. "Huey—where are you?"

Every nerve in my body was tingling as I continued to call Huey's name. It had been five and a half hours since I had left the house that morning. Five and a half hours of unrelenting wind and snow. It was so cold my face was already stinging. How could he possibly survive this?

"Huey!" I called out again. "Come on, Huey! Please!"

At first my frantic shouts were greeted with silence. But after five minutes of repeatedly calling out Huey's name, I heard a faint meow mixed with the howling winter storm.

My heart leaped as I leaped into the snow, trying to determine where the sound was coming from.

"Huey!" I shouted again, pushing my way toward the street. "I'm here. Come on, Huey."

The meows grew louder, telling me I was moving in the right direction. I continued to follow his sounds to a large commercial dumpster, where I found him huddled underneath, trapped by the snow.

I dropped to my knees, shoved the snow out of the way, and reached my arms underneath the dumpster.

"Don't worry, Huey, I've got you," I managed as I scooped his trembling body into my arms.

I rushed him into the house, wrapped him in a blanket, pulled him against my chest, and rocked him until his shaking stopped.

Within a couple of hours, he was back to his normal self, but the realization that I had almost lost him was so terrifying that I didn't want to let him out of my arms. I vowed to never again let him get in harm's way. But it seemed like trauma and danger had been stamped into his DNA.

The night that will forever be seared in my mind started with a barbeque on my apartment deck.

Huey and I had moved into the apartment unit eleven days earlier, after I had made the decision to sell my house, pay off some debt I had accrued, and make a fresh start.

It had been a long day at work and I just wanted it to be

over. I forced myself to stop by the store for a few groceries, had thrown a steak on my patio grill, and then had vegged in front of my TV with Huey on my lap before crawling into bed.

I'm not sure when I dozed off or how long I had been asleep before a man's shouts jolted me awake.

"If anyone is here, you've got to get out now! Your place is on fire."

Everything registered at once. There was a man standing in my bedroom doorway and the smell of smoke filling my room. A fire alarm was ringing from the hallway and I could hear the shrill beeps from my smoke detector coming from my living room.

"Come on!" the man yelled. "We've got to get out of here now!"

I jumped out of my bed and rushed toward the door. I was only wearing boxer shorts, but the smoke was pouring into my room and I knew we were almost out of time.

We made it to my apartment door when I remembered Huey. My living room and kitchen area were now consumed by flames and smoke, and I knew that he was somewhere in the middle of it.

"Huey," I frantically called. "Come on, Huey. Please!"

My rescuer, who I later learned was my neighbor, grabbed me by my arm and started dragging me out the door.

"We're going! Now!" he yelled.

He pulled me into the smoke-filled hallway and began guiding us to the stairs just as a couple of firemen pushed past us.

A mix of helplessness and rage surged through me and I lost it. My hands balled into fists that punched holes through the sheetrock as we pushed our way down the steps. Huey was burning to death. And I had no way to help him.

By the time we made it to the safety of the parking lot, the entire apartment complex was engulfed in flames. I stood in silence with the other tenants, watching our lives turn to ash. For a few minutes, I was too shocked to feel anything. Then it hit me: I had nothing. No home, no money, no possessions, no Huey.

My mind kicked into survival mode. I had a friend, Gail, who lived in a condo a block from my apartment complex, and I sprinted to her building.

I rang her doorbell, then remembered that the only thing I had on were my boxers. I quickly dodged behind her car so she wouldn't see me.

"Gail. It's Randy. I need help," I called out as soon as she opened the door. "My apartment is burning down and I have nothing—not even clothes."

Within minutes, Gail was by my side, handing me a T-shirt and $80. I thanked her, pulled on the T-shirt, and headed the five blocks to Daryl's house.

It was nearly eleven p.m. when I knocked on his door and I knew he was probably asleep. But I had nowhere else to go.

"What's going on, buddy?" he asked, eyeing me with concern as he ushered me inside.

My body shook as I blurted the words. "My apartment is on fire and I need a place to stay."

I spent the next few days trapped in a growing nightmare. I could hear what I envisioned were Huey's desperate meows for help as the fire and smoke engulfed him. It was so painful to think about Huey suffering that I would quickly force the thoughts from my mind, only to be hit with the reminder that I was homeless and had lost everything I owned. As if that wasn't bad enough, I was facing a possible $1.3 million liability charge because, according to the fire marshal, the fire—which had destroyed twenty-six apartment units—had started in my apartment.

"It either started from your grill or your halogen lamp," he told me after calling me in for an investigative interview. "Either way, it originated in your apartment."

I had been smart enough to carry personal property insurance and though I had let it lapse for the eleven days I had been in my new place, I discovered that it miraculously came with a thirty-day grace period—enabling me to reinstate it for $168.

This gave me a million dollars in liability coverage. But I was still $300,000 short.

I was a thirty-six-year-old bachelor who worked as a pressman. I had no way to get my hands on that kind of money. My rational self held out hope that a settlement could be reached with the insurance company. But then anxiety and fear would take over and I worried that I would be left with only one choice: to flee the country.

Three days after the fire, I was finally given the clearance to go back into my apartment to search for anything of value.

I had been mentally preparing myself for the disaster I would find. But the one thing I couldn't wrap my head around was the loss of Huey.

"Have you found his remains?" I asked the fire marshal, bracing myself for his response.

I could see the empathy in his eyes as he shook his head.

"No, I'm sorry," he said. "I wouldn't give up hope, though. Cats are extremely tough and I've seen them survive worse."

I didn't think Huey stood a chance of surviving a fire that had consumed twenty-six apartment units. But I knew he was trying to make me feel better and I appreciated his words.

As I turned to leave, the fire marshal reached into a desk drawer and pulled out my apartment keys. "We found these," he said as he handed them to me.

I don't know what I was expecting—at least a melted key

ring or something. But my keys didn't have a smudge on them.

When I expressed my amazement at this, the fire marshal smiled.

"That's because you left them in your door," he said. "That's how your neighbor was able to let himself in to get to you."

I was stunned. I'd had several bags of groceries in my arms when I was opening the door and must have been so exhausted and overwhelmed that I had forgotten to retrieve my keys. I had never done that before. But had I not left them in the lock, it was likely I wouldn't have made it out.

My mom had flown in from Vancouver to help me and the two of us headed into the apartment together to see if there was anything worth salvaging. The place was a pile of debris and ash. Yet two things jumped out: On the kitchen counter was a roll of paper towels that hadn't been touched. And on top of the TV, which was completely melted, was my wallet, still intact, with $200 in cash beneath it.

I headed to my bedroom to see if any of my clothes had made it through. My entire wardrobe was still hanging in my walk-in closet, covered in ash and reeking of smoke.

I grabbed a couple pairs of shoes and pulled out a box of storage items from my closet floor. That's when I saw Huey curled in the corner, covered in ash.

My heart dropped to my gut.

I gently rested my hand on Huey's ash-covered coat, my body trembling as the grief and sadness took hold. Huey had been the one constant in my life for the past five years. He had been there for me every day, showering me with his unconditional love and reminding me that I was never alone. And now he was gone.

I could feel the hole opening up inside me as I buried my hand deeper into his fur. That's when his beautiful yellow eyes suddenly opened and looked at me. Before I could consciously register what was happening, I had Huey cradled against my chest.

"He's ALIVE!" I shouted to my mom. "He's ALIVE."

Within seconds, his paws were on my shoulders and he was nursing on my earlobe as though nothing had happened.

In that moment it didn't matter that I was homeless or that I might have to flee the country to avoid the $300,000 charge. I had my family back.

The apartment owners eventually settled for the million dollars the insurance company paid out, and Huey and I were able to rebuild our lives. We enjoyed nine more years together before cancer finally took him down. I sobbed like a baby when I had to put him to sleep, and when I buried him, I buried a piece of my heart.

The only part of Huey that remained was his blanket, which I kept near my pillow. I wasn't sure that I had the capacity to love another cat. But the deafening silence and loneliness in the weeks that followed his death had been so intense I knew I had to fill the void. And that's how Conway came into my life.

Conway wasn't Huey. But he had brought his own spunk and quirky personality into our relationship and we had forged our own bond. Like Huey, Conway was my family. And no matter what happened in my external world, I knew I could always count on him.

11

I was back at my log-cabin house two weeks later, soaking up more Conway time while enjoying a relaxing evening with Dave and Shirley, when the conversation turned to Jeremy.

"He is really doing great," Dave gushed. "I was just telling my brother the other day about his houses and office building. It's amazing."

It was a casual, off-the-cuff comment from a dad who was clearly proud of his son and seemed to be unaware of the facts. But given the enormity of the mischaracterization—combined with the title stunt Jeremy had pulled two months earlier—his words came at me like a torpedo.

"Whoa, Dave. Hold on," I said, struggling to maintain my composure. "I bought the houses and office building. They are mine. They are collateral until the company assets are worth the equivalent or more of my investment."

Though I had given Jeremy a pass on the way he handled the titles, nothing had changed from an ownership perspective. The mobile software app was coming along according to plan, but no sales had been made yet and the company wasn't anywhere near being cash-flow equivalent to my investment. There wasn't cash flowing at all.

I wanted to give Jeremy the benefit of the doubt, but I had been on alert ever since the incident and had a nagging sense that something was off.

My mind began racing, recounting every small warning flag that had presented itself. The most recent had popped up during my last visit to Scottsdale a few weeks earlier.

As usual, I had stayed with Jeremy's family, and the evening I arrived he walked me to his garage, saying he had something to show me.

"Take a look at this," he said, motioning inside.

There, sitting in the over-sized garage, was a 1999 Ferrari F355 Spider. The car was a beauty. And I knew it was expensive.

"Dude, where did you get this?" I asked.

Jeremy shrugged. "Oh, I sold some shares I had from another company," he replied.

It had sounded a little suspicious, but I figured it was his right to sell some of his stock.

But it had nagged at me because I knew how broke Jeremy had been, and it seemed irresponsible to be purchasing expensive sports cars when money was so tight and the company was still months away from generating any revenue.

A swarm of fire ants filled my insides as my mind tallied the mounting red flags. I knew how much Dave loved and idolized Jeremy. But if something wasn't on the up-and-up, I needed to know now.

"Dave," I started in a tentative voice, "I'm sorry to ask this because I know he's your son. But is there something I should know about Jeremy?"

Dave didn't seem fazed by my question. Instead he smiled, moved toward me, and put his arm around my shoulder.

"You know, Randy, I don't understand everything my son does," he said. "I know he's a little different, but talent comes in all packages. All I can tell you is that he's building a rocket ship."

Dave's reassurance washed over me, and I could feel my body temperature beginning to cool. He was one of my closest friends, and if he was telling me that everything was fine with Jeremy, then he must be right. On top of that, he had essentially reiterated what the programmers at the Nerdery had told me—that Jeremy had nailed the application and had so brilliantly integrated social media and customer loyalty with the touch, tag, and purchase capabilities, that KULTiD was going to change the face of ecommerce.

Shirley, who had been listening to our exchange, joined in.

"Randy, you have nothing to worry about with Jeremy," she said, locking her eyes on mine. "He's a good Christian and we raised him right. Jeremy wouldn't steal a dime from anyone. He is the last person in the world you have to worry about."

Her interjection diffused any remaining concerns. Everything about Shirley calmed me. She was in her early sixties, with curly grey hair, a warm smile and such a sincere presence she reminded me of a small-town grandmother.

Like with the titles, I let myself get talked off the ledge. But the nagging feeling didn't go away and kicked up a notch when I received an email from Jeremy in mid-September asking for another $1 million investment in exchange for an additional one percent in the company. He said he needed the money to acquire more office space and increase staffing.

"It's God's vision," he wrote in his email pitch, referencing his faith as he often did in our conversations.

As always, he provided a glowing report on the skyrocketing excitement surrounding KULTiD and the increasing company valuation. But something didn't sit right with me. The company was still in start-up mode, with only a handful of staff, an office building that was already paid for, and a software app that I had fully funded from a development perspective. On top of that, I had just delivered the fourth $500,000 installment to cover operating expenses. It seemed inconceivable that the money was already gone.

We were now only six weeks away from the company launch party and, based on the reports I was getting from both Jeremy and Ross, I expected it to take off immediately. But I was done being the money tree.

"I'm sorry, Jeremy," I replied. "I've reached my ceiling."

Within minutes, Jeremy was on the phone, pushing back.

"Listen, we are so close," he said. "This money will get us to the finish line."

When I held firm, Jeremy switched gears.

"Well, what if you were to invest in my other software project?" he started, briefly outlining his newest vision.

His idea—Medicare payment tracking software that integrated with systems in all fifty states—sounded promising. But we hadn't even made it to the official starting line for the KULTiD app. Jeremy was like a kid in a candy store grabbing for the next piece of candy before he had even unwrapped the first one.

"We haven't even gotten KULTiD off the ground," I replied, struggling to contain my exasperation. "Let's do one thing at a time and do it right. Then we can talk about the next project."

Jeremy continued to push over the next few days, arguing that our market opportunity was now and that we would miss out if we didn't jump on it. But my internal brakes had kicked in and nothing was going to sway me.

"I'm sorry, Jeremy, but I'm done," I repeated. "I've reached my limit."

A week later, he sent a text saying that he had just met an

investor who agreed to put up the entire $10 million he needed for the next round of funding for both KULTiD and the other game-changing software KULT Labs was developing. He explained that the man, whom he said he had met on a flight, had just sold a company for $650 million and was looking for a start-up in which to invest.

His pronouncement sounded so miraculous and unlikely that I couldn't help but question it.

"He just agreed to invest ten million dollars on the spot without doing any due diligence?" I asked.

"Yes!" Jeremy replied.

It sounded fishy but if someone was really willing to slap down that kind of money, without doing any research into the company or its financials, that was his business. And if it was really true, I was glad to know someone other than me was kicking in some capital. The sooner this software was out into the marketplace, the sooner I would be able to recoup my investment and start generating returns.

"Well, that's great, Jeremy," I replied. "I'm happy for you."

12

DESPITE THE GROWING LUMP IN my gut and an internal voice that was screaming otherwise, I was still clinging to the hope that everything was okay with KULTiD. But that went out the window the second I took in Jeremy's face.

It was late October and we were sitting in a booth at a Scottsdale restaurant, having a business lunch meeting with Ross Richardson, Jacob, and Michael DeRaffel, a COO Jeremy had recently brought on board.

I had been in town for a week, waiting for the November 1 launch party. And after everything I had seen and heard, I knew I needed answers.

Jeremy had started badgering me for money almost the instant I arrived in town, explaining that the $10 million investment he had told me about hadn't yet come through and he was in dire need of operating capital. Yet when I stopped by the KULT Labs office building the following morning, I saw two new Porsches—a Carrera 4 convertible and a Cayenne

Turbo S—sitting in the company driveway.

I didn't have to ask to know that these vehicles—which easily cost $200,000—had been purchased by Jeremy. I knew it with every part of my being. And after all the pleading, begging, and strong-arming he had employed over the past five weeks to get me to invest more money, I knew that it was my $2 million cash infusion that had been used to finance those cars.

Every cell in my body was on fire as I stepped into the office to confront Jeremy.

"I just saw the cars. What is going on?" I demanded as soon as I found him.

Jeremy shot me a look that was half-defiant, half-pleading as he spewed the same sob story he had given me when he demanded that I fly Amy to Hawaii during our meetings in April.

"I nearly lost Amy to lupus and these cars have always been a dream of hers," he said.

I had crumbled back then, but this time I wasn't falling for his crap. It was inconceivable to me that he could try to justify such a blatant misuse of my investment with a straight face.

"Jeremy, we are not cash flowing," I thundered. "We have got to watch spending."

He didn't respond, but I wasn't letting this one go. I immediately headed to Ross's office for answers.

As the Chief Financial Officer, Ross was supposed to be the money watchdog and make sure all expenditures were appropriate.

I hoped he would clarify things and somehow ease my concern. But when I confronted him, he came up with his own ridiculous excuse.

"I know, Randy, he really had to talk me into this," Ross said, as though his hesitation made it okay. "But I've made him sign an accountability clause with me."

I left that encounter feeling queasy. A slow, steady panic had been building inside me for a couple of months now and had been escalating since Jeremy's pressure to invest more money began in mid-September. I was a big picture guy, but day-to-day operations were not my strong suit and I was horrible at accounting.

I knew I was in over my head, both with KULT Labs and my overall management of the enormous amount of money I had been given. I needed professionals to guide me so I didn't end up losing everything I had.

This realization had hit me during my drive to Scottsdale and I had immediately started assembling a team of guys I knew and trusted. There were three in all: my friend, Trevor, who knew marketing inside and out; Max, a seasoned accountant I knew from my days in Edmonton; and Mike, a man I had recently befriended who was a pro at operations.

I had invited them all to the launch party and asked them to come a couple of days early so they could do some digging and get a clear snapshot of current KULTiD financials, the go-to-market plan, and both the short-term and long-term revenue projections.

Despite the clear mismanagement and overspending, I hoped it was just a matter of rookie mistakes that could be corrected if I brought in a team of seasoned professionals to guide the company.

I had asked for the lunch meeting with Jeremy and the rest of the KULTiD management team so I could begin getting a handle on the situation. I wanted to keep it professional, but I was also done with the vague answers I had been getting.

We were seated in a horseshoe booth with Jeremy in my direct line of sight, so I started with him.

"Jeremy," I said, "we need to talk about how we are going to structure cash flow and recapture my investment."

As usual, he deflected my questions.

"There are a lot of things to discuss because we need more investments for research and development."

I could feel my insides boiling. In the week since I had been in town, Jeremy had continued to pressure me for more money to cover operating costs, even breaking down in tears at one point. He had worked me over so much that I had briefly considered another collateral-based investment of a million dollars, only to have Ross and Jeremy present me with a document that listed my office building and the Scottsdale house as the collateral.

It was so outrageous it was beyond offensive—it was almost laughable.

"Are you kidding me?" I had barked. "Those assets are already mine!"

I waited for Ross to jump into the conversation and offer some sort of realistic financial projections that we could anticipate once the software launched. Instead, he dug into his food and kept silent.

I fought back the rage making its way up my throat and forced my voice to remain calm and in control.

"That's fine, Jeremy," I replied, keeping my eyes locked on his, "but my accountant and the rest of my business team are coming down and they are going to want answers."

It was as though my words had triggered a bomb inside of him. In a flash, the color of his face turned to magenta, and there was so much rage in his eyes I could feel the heat. Almost instantly, his face returned to normal. But I knew there was nothing normal about what was going on. The air had suddenly turned cold and none of the team had responded to my requests for information.

"As I mentioned, my team will be here soon," I reiterated to everyone as we got up to leave. "You all are going to get to know them very well."

❖

Thirty hours later I was sitting in front-row seats at the Coyotes ice hockey game with Trevor and Mike.

The season ticket seats, four in all, came with a KULT Labs reserved sign, another in-my-face reminder that the money I had invested was being wasted. But what was even more disturbing was that Jeremy and the rest of the KULT Lab crew and their families were partying it up in a luxury box—which I also knew I was inadvertently financing—and I hadn't even been invited.

Jeremy had mentioned that he had rented the luxury box for the game several days earlier and I had assumed that I would be there with Trevor and Mike. But that morning, he had handed me the tickets for the seats, explaining there just wasn't room for us.

"These are better anyway," he added, as though I was an idiot that didn't know better. "They are right on the ice."

It was a clear slap in the face, but I had tried to excuse it in my mind and be civil.

"Okay, well, then come down and meet my guys when you get a chance," I had said.

I waited for him to appear the entire first period, but hadn't even heard from him.

I could see the disgust in Trevor's eyes whenever I looked at him, and I knew Mike was upset. He already had a bad taste in his mouth, because earlier that day we had stopped by the office so I could introduce him to Ross and had found him kicking back with his feet on his desk, listening to YouTube music videos. If that wasn't bad enough, within minutes of my arrival in his office, Ross was hitting me up for a million dollars to invest in one of his own ventures.

I fired off a text to Jeremy.

"Hey, man, where are you? My guys flew all the way in from Canada. I want you to come down and meet them."

His reply was short and dismissive. "Sorry. Our wives are here and we can't leave them."

It was such a ridiculous response I had to fight the urge to storm up to the box and break down the door. I knew Shirley was up there with them. She and Dave had been flown in on company funds. Yet, not only was she not intervening on my behalf, she was joining in on dissing me. I was in a deepening nightmare that I couldn't escape.

"Listen, you are disrespecting us," I pounded out on my cell phone keyboard. "At least come down at the break to say a quick hello."

I spent most of the game seething—trying to fathom how they could think it was okay to treat me like this. Without me, no one up in that box would even have a job. What's more, Shirley and Dave certainly wouldn't be living in a million-dollar house and getting paid generously to look after it. Yet now that I had turned off the money faucet and was beginning to ask questions, I was being treated like trash.

When Jeremy refused to even meet up with us for a drink after the game, I had sent another text to him and Ross, insisting that they meet with us for breakfast the following morning.

But a few minutes before we were set to meet, Ross sent a text canceling on us.

The line had been drawn. As far as I was concerned, it was now a matter of documenting evidence of the enormous mismanagement to support my taking over the company.

"Let's go to the office to see what we can find out," I said to Trevor and Mike.

I had been so caught up in the excitement of it all that I

hadn't paid much attention to office furnishings. But the minute Trevor saw the custom carpet and large-screen color TVs still in their boxes, he came unglued.

"What is going on here?" he snapped.

He and Mike immediately began taking pictures to document the waste—including new, unused workstations equipped with $3,000 Mac computers.

Though I managed to maintain a calm, composed demeanor, I felt like I had just been gutted. I had sung Jeremy's praises to all of my friends over the past five months, talking him up as the next Steve Jobs. Because of Dave and Shirley's assurances, I had put my complete trust in their son. Because of my love for Dave and my belief that he and Shirley had my back, I had turned over a tenth of my winnings to help relieve Jeremy's personal financial stress and get KULTiD off the ground, and I had ignored all of the obvious warning signs.

Now, here we were, a day before the launch party that would officially kick off KULTiD and unveil the software to the world, and everything was going south. In my excitement, I had invited Brent and a few other friends to come down for the event. It was supposed to be my big day, the day I had raved about and anticipated for months. And everything was going up in flames.

We wrapped up our tour of the office and headed back to the W Hotel for a strategy session. Max and my attorney had arrived and after filling them in on the situation, we devised a plan of attack.

"Listen," I said as we gathered in the hotel bar for a drink. "Their cat and mouse game is coming to an end. They can't avoid us at the launch party and they can't keep us out. That's where we are going to get to the bottom of this."

13

THE LAUNCH PARTY KICKED OFF at four p.m. with red carpet treatment and photographers snapping pictures of the guests as they arrived at the W Hotel.

We walked the carpet and got our pictures taken and then waited for Jeremy and Amy to arrive. They pulled up in the Turbo S my money had financed and tried to avoid us as they walked the carpet.

"We need to talk, Jeremy," I said as soon as he was within earshot.

I could see Amy stiffen. As usual, she was meticulously dressed with carefully applied make-up that made her piercing blue eyes pop. Her dark hair hugged her thin, almost gaunt, frame that was magnified by Jeremy's stocky build.

"I don't have time for that," he hissed, moving toward the elevator that would take him to the rooftop party.

The plan I had devised with my team, which I had officially dubbed the Rush Group, was a simple divide-and-conquer strategy. Mike and my attorney would corner Jeremy, while

Trevor and Max teamed up on Ross. Amid it all, they would be circulating among the crowd at the party, listening to conversations, asking questions, and discerning who was there.

We made our way up to the rooftop deck, where the party was beginning to get underway. I kept an eye out for the local media that Jeremy had promised would be there to capture the story and spread the word about KULTiD, but not a single news outlet was there. Nor were any of the celebrities Jeremy had promised. All I could see besides the KULT-branded beach balls floating in the pool were a bunch of promotional models Jeremy had hired, intermixed with freeloaders getting their fill of overpriced cocktails and hors d'oeuvres.

The event kicked off with a short welcoming speech by Ross and a software presentation by Jeremy and Amy.

I had been waiting for this moment ever since Jeremy had told me that the software had been approved by Apple. But when Jeremy tried to walk people through the app, I could hear grumbling among some of the guests.

"It doesn't seem to be working completely," one person remarked.

"Yeah, and it only works on IOS systems. It doesn't work on Androids," another added.

This last comment alarmed Trevor, who had plenty of experience with mobile apps.

"This doesn't smell right," he said, the dismay apparent on his face. "It's much less expensive and much easier to launch an Android app—and they make up the majority of the marketplace. If anything, that should have been done first."

As I took in this information, I waited for Jeremy to mention the apparel manufacturers that KULTiD was supposedly going to be partnering with. Without merchandise to sell through the app, there was no viable revenue model. But there was no mention. Nor, as far as we could tell, were there any apparel or merchandise manufacturers even in attendance. Everyone my guys talked with were either family or friends of Jeremy, Ross, and other staff members.

Jeremy wrapped up his presentation without a single reference to me or any acknowledgment that it was thanks to my capital infusion that the company had even gotten off the ground. While I was simmering over that, I noticed Dave. He was about ten feet in front of me and was about to pass by.

Like Jeremy, he and Shirley had gone out of their way to avoid me since their arrival in town a week before, and I had had enough.

"Hello, Dave," I called out as I walked toward him.

Dave let out a nervous laugh.

"Oh, hello, brother," he replied, acting like he was surprised to see me.

It was hard to fathom that this was the same man I loved so much that I had planned to financially support him for the rest of his life. It was as though I was talking with a stranger.

"How long have you been in town?" I asked, already knowing the answer but wanting to hear his response.

Dave took a gulp of his drink.

"Oh, we got here a few days ago," he replied, avoiding eye contact with me.

It had been impossible not to know about his whereabouts for the past week, because Jeremy was obsessive about posting photos on Facebook. They showed Dave and Shirley living it up at a private dinner with Jeremy and the rest of the KULTiD team, as well as at breakfast with everyone the day before—at the same time Jeremy and Ross were supposed to be meeting with me and my team.

"So why didn't you text or reach out?" I pushed. "You knew I was in town."

I could feel Dave's discomfort, and at this point, I welcomed it. I wanted him to squirm. Whatever was going on with Jeremy, it was clear to me from Dave's behavior that he wasn't an innocent bystander. What I was having a difficult time grasping was why he would jeopardize a situation that had been so good for him.

A few days after winning the lottery and stopping by Dave's house to share my news and offer him a free place to live and a monthly stipend, I had called him with another surprise.

"I want you to meet me at the bike shop," I told him. "I want you to pick out whatever bike you want."

Dave was obsessed with motorcycles and it felt amazing to be able to give him such a meaningful gift. He spent a few minutes looking at different models before picking out the most expensive motorbike in the shop, a $32,000 Indian.

"You don't mind, do you, brother?" he asked sheepishly.

I was a little taken aback because, had our roles been reversed, I would have erred on the side of least expensive. But I shook the feeling off.

"It's fine, Dave," I replied. "Go for it."

After paying for the bike, I spontaneously pulled out my checkbook and wrote out a check to him for $25,000.

Dave looked at me in disbelief. I saw tears pool in his eyes.

"You have no idea what this means to us, brother," he said as he pocketed the check. "Shirley and I are facing bankruptcy and this is exactly the amount we owe."

I had been inspired to write him that check and was thrilled that it provided him with the money he so desperately needed.

I hadn't thought any more of it until I was in Honolulu with Brent and his family two months later—where I'd headed after my business powwow in Hawaii with Jeremy and Trevor.

We were relaxing at the beach outside the Outrigger Hotel when I received a phone call from him.

"Brother, we are in Maui," he said. "Shirley and I decided to take a vacation and wondered if we could come over and meet up with you for a few days."

Given the dire situation he'd expressed just a few weeks earlier, it surprised me that he was splurging on such an expensive vacation. As though he had read my mind, Dave explained that he had taken some of the bankruptcy money and used it for the trip.

It sounded irresponsible to me, but I figured he was the steward of the money I had provided and could choose to spend it how he wanted.

"Sure, come on over," I had replied. "I'd love to see you. I'll get you a room at the hotel."

The sound of the DJ—the one Jeremy had flown in from Canada exclusively for the launch party—snapped me back to the present.

I left Dave and made my way back to Max and Trevor. Minutes later my attorney came charging toward me. It took only one look at him to know that something was seriously wrong.

But I still wasn't prepared for the blow he delivered.

The words "Jeremy says it's all his—he says you have nothing," ricocheted through my brain like a bullet.

I was spinning and felt like I was freefalling down a dark, never-ending hole.

The next few minutes were a blur. Somewhere in the middle of it I had a heated exchange with Jeremy before being escorted by Trevor to the hotel conference room Mike had secured so we could get a handle on things and begin devising a game plan.

I could hear the jumble of voices erupting around me as my team began to strategize. But I was so shaken I couldn't hear what they were saying.

I had let my heart and love for Dave lead me. And he had delivered me up on a silver platter, all the while acting like my best friend and a deeply committed Christian. He was his own form of Judas.

My thoughts jumped to a conversation I'd had with Jeremy the day I had landed in Scottsdale a week and a half earlier. Though my concerns were building, we were still on decent terms and at that point, I still had every reason to believe KULTiD was headed for success—especially after Jeremy showed me that the software app was live on Apple. Then Jeremy steered the conversation to Dave and Shirley.

"Listen, Randy—I've been thinking about this and really want to retire my parents."

His words came out of left field.

"What do you mean?" I replied. "They are retired. I've retired them."

Jeremy had shot me a look of disgust—as if providing them with a free place to live in a million-dollar house and paying them a generous monthly stipend was akin to a garbage dump.

"That's not what I mean," he had pushed. "I want to retire them in style."

It had left a bad taste in my mouth but I had chalked it up to one of Jeremy's off-the-cuff comments. Now I wondered if Dave and Shirley had put him up to it—hoping they could weasel more money out of me.

That thought snapped me out of my shock. They had played me hard, but now it was my turn and there was no way I was going to let them get away with this.

An inferno was now burning inside of me, fueling me with an intensity that nearly matched my lottery win. Emotions had gotten me into this mess. But they were also going to get me out of it. And I knew I had the team in place to help me do it.

"Let's shut the company down," I said, feeling a surge of power as I spoke. "Then let's strip Jeremy and anyone else involved of everything they've got."

14

Dave and Jeremy might have pegged me as a naive, bighearted guy who could be taken advantage of and wouldn't fight back.

But there was another side ingrained deep within my DNA and upbringing, and they had just unleashed it.

The first time my revenge gene kicked in happened in third grade.

A few weeks earlier, I had spotted a must-have Road Runner lunch box in a general merchandise store while shopping with my mom. We didn't have the money for such luxuries so I went to work, combing the streets and garbage bins throughout our neighborhood in search of soda cans and Coca-Cola bottles that I redeemed for cash.

When I finally had enough money to purchase it, that shiny Road Runner lunch box—featuring an image of the Road Runner and his famous "Beep Beep" line—was my most prized possession. I couldn't wait to show it off at school, but my joy was quickly sapped by Peter and Ricky, fourth- and fifth-grade bullies.

"Beep, beep, my ass," they taunted, flanking either side of me and giving me a shove.

The bullying continued the next day, with the same "beep, beep, my ass" taunt, followed by a more aggressive shove. Within a week, the taunts had escalated to a punch in the stomach.

The bullying and abuse went on for nearly a month before I finally broke down and reported the situation to my mom. But when she brought it to the attention of my principal and teacher, they shrugged it off.

"Kids will be kids," was my teacher's only reply.

New Westminster wasn't the kind of town where boys showed weakness. Gangs roamed the streets looking for trouble, and guys went all out to make a name for themselves. If you presented as weak, you became easy prey.

My mother knew this all too well, and while she beat manners into me from as early as I could remember, she was also adamant that I stand my ground.

"The next time they bother you, give them everything you've got," she stressed.

It was two against one, and they were both older and bigger than me. But when they cornered me at lunch the following day and started in on their "Beep, beep, my ass" taunt, I was ready.

I swung my lunch box at Peter's face as hard as I could and smashed it into his forehead. The metal edge must have caught him, because it left a large gash that sent blood spurting and landed Peter in the hospital for stitches. For the first time in a month, I felt strong and empowered.

I was suspended for three days but was never bullied again. Even so, I didn't let it go. I still hadn't gotten back at Ricky, and when I saw him at a baseball game seven years later, the same rage and need for revenge took over.

"Beep, beep, my ass!" I barked, getting in his face. "Remember me?"

Before he could answer, I swung at his head, knocking him to the ground.

"Remember me now?" I sneered.

❖

Like most of my friends, my childhood was shaped by welfare, violence, alcoholism, and crime. And between that environment and my strong genetic disposition, my need to fight back and get even when I or anyone else I cared for had been wronged was a given.

I didn't know my biological dad, but I knew from my mom that he was a career criminal who lived by his own code of right and wrong and took matters into his own hands whenever he believed an injustice had occurred.

Though I was too young to remember, my mom told me that her first husband, Richard Philbrook, was a violent alcoholic who constantly beat on her. When word got around to my dad, she told me he went berserk.

"We were having a party at our house and your dad called to ask if he could swing by," my mom recounted on several occasions. "He showed up with five or six guys and began wasting people.

"One guy went out the window and Richard ended up with a broken jaw that had to be wired shut," she continued, always laughing when she got to this part of the story. "I went to his hospital room the next day with divorce papers. He signed them on the spot and never bothered us again."

The story was so matter-of-fact and such a normal part of my everyday life that I didn't think anything of it. Of course my dad busted Richard's jaw and beat the crap out of him. He had it coming.

No one in my neighborhood waited for the justice system to intervene when they had been wronged. I'm sure part of this had to do with the vigilante mentality that ruled the streets. But an even bigger reason for not turning to law enforcement for help was because most everyone I grew up around was involved in some sort of criminal activity. The people I knew—unlike Dave and Jeremy—were upfront about their crimes. They didn't pretend to be saints and didn't develop fake friendships so they could gain someone's trust and then con them out of their money. They took it outright. They would never have considered screwing over someone they professed to love.

Given my genes, my surroundings, and my early role models, it was as though I was being groomed for a life of crime myself.

The first father figure I remember was my mom's common-law husband, Victor, a gregarious Hungarian who had escaped the revolution. Victor, who was eleven years older than my mom, and, like her, was on welfare, was a small-time crook who was always on the lookout for an easy score.

One night when I was ten, he decided to involve me. A few weeks earlier, some thugs had broken into a house a few blocks from our apartment and assaulted the elderly woman who lived there, sending her to the hospital.

This meant the house was empty, which Victor viewed as an opportunity.

"Go over there and check it out," he directed.

Adrenaline coursed through me as I headed to the ancient, hundred-year-old property.

I crept around the side of the house in the dark black of night, looking for an easy entrance. After several tries, I found a window that wasn't locked, pushed it up, and climbed through.

There wasn't much to be found, just some old furniture

and a few boxes. But I rummaged through some drawers and discovered a stack of old postcards, letters, and stamps, which I figured could be of value.

I stuffed them into my coat pocket and was halfway out the window when I felt a hand on my leg.

"I got you!" a man's voice barked in my ear.

Panic gripped me as the police officer walked me to his car and demanded to know where I lived.

"What were you doing in there?" he chided as he drove toward my apartment. "That's breaking and entering and is a serious crime. Let's see what your parents have to say about this."

The only thought running through my mind was what Victor was going to do when he learned that I had been caught.

The police officer escorted me to my apartment door, asked to come inside, and proceeded to tell Victor about my bad behavior.

I could see the concern on Victor's face and his constant glares at me as he assured the police officer that I would never do that again.

I concentrated on breathing, bracing myself for what was to come.

But when the cop was gone, Victor only had one question for me.

"Did you rat me out?"

Even at the age of ten, I understood enough to know that if you got caught for something you shouldn't be doing, you took the heat no matter who else was involved.

"No, of course not," I replied defiantly.

His answer was short and to the point. "Good."

❖

By the time I was fifteen, I was a rowdy, long-haired punk convinced that I was on my way to an early death. I ran with an out-of-control group of guys and spent my free time drinking, smoking pot, and taking LSD. My friends were beginning to rack up arrest sheets for breaking and entering, theft, and drug sales. They burglarized houses and once even went as far as breaking into our high school and stealing all of the computers.

Though I managed to steer clear of any serious trouble by following my inner guide—which told me when it was time to leave a party or avoid getting into a car—I was crossing an increasingly blurry line. Given the direction my life was going, I seemed destined to follow in my dad's footsteps.

Aside from my two brief encounters with him when I was a young kid and the occasional stories my mom had told me, I knew nothing about my dad. But that changed with the news my friend's father dropped on me when I was a sophomore in high school.

I was hanging out at Fenton's house after school one day drinking beer when his dad arrived home from work.

"Got a cold one for the old man?" he asked, joining our conversation.

My mom had raised me to be polite and engaging so I began asking him questions about himself. When I asked what he did for a living, Fenton's dad—a burly, rough-looking man—said he was a longshoreman.

That piqued my interest and gave me something more to talk about.

"That's cool. Both my grandfathers and my dad are longshoremen as well," I responded, repeating information I had learned from my mom.

Fenton's dad looked at me curiously.

"Oh, yeah? Who's your old man?"

Though I didn't know him, pride bubbled inside me as I

answered, "Glen Wells."

The look on his face went from curious to disbelief.

"You are Glen Wells's son?" he said. "You know he's dead, right? He was killed a couple of years ago after getting caught in a huge drug bust."

His words ricocheted through me. My dad was just a name and a few stories I had heard over the years. I didn't feel a connection with him because he had never been part of my life. But it was still a shock.

My mom didn't believe me when I recounted the information I had been given. But several months later, while attending a neighborhood Christmas party, I overheard her talking with a man who confirmed it. My dad had been gunned down while awaiting trial after being arrested in the biggest heroin smuggling bust in Vancouver to date.

❖

Most of my friends were on a downward spiral and I might have followed them had it not been for the fear of my stepfather's wrath.

My mom married Steve, an immigrant from Czechoslovakia, when I was eleven. Like the rest of us, Steve was no stranger to violence.

He had grown up under harsh Communist rule, and an even harsher stepfather—a raging alcoholic who constantly beat up on his mother.

A month before Steve escaped to Canada, he walked in on his stepdad pummeling his mom and was so overcome with rage that he kicked him in the mouth, knocking out most of his teeth.

Steve, who had taken me on as his own son, liked to have fun and was good to both my mom and me. But he had an explosive temper and when I got even a little bit out of line, he didn't mess around.

Unlike Victor, Steve was an honest, hardworking guy who had no tolerance for misbehavior, and his violence terrified me. At first, he used his belt on me. Once, knowing what was coming, I headed to my room and put on eight pairs of underwear to soften the blows—only to be found out—and I got twelve lashes on my bare butt instead. The belt was bad, but it was nothing compared to the open-hand palm strike he started using on me when I became a teenager. His temper, when ignited, was so lethal that I walked on eggshells, scared to death of getting caught on the wrong side of his eruptions. The worst and last time happened when I was seventeen. It was a cold Saturday afternoon and the two of us were home, sorting through storage boxes. Maybe I made a snide remark about having to spend my Saturday that way. I can't remember. But what will forever be seared in my mind is his open-hand palm strike smashing into my face. Even before the pain registered, I could see stars and hear ringing in my ears.

"Don't you ever disrespect me like that again," I heard Steve barking somewhere amidst the fog. I was too stunned and scared to speak. I just stood there until everything inside my head settled and then bolted for the door. The hit he delivered, which he later admitted was his knockout punch, landed with so much force it knocked one of my molars loose.

My fear of Steve's rage—which my mom had a unique ability to fuel—was a definite deterrent when it came to engaging in the criminal activities my friends were now pursuing.

But it was the encouraging, uplifting words from a friend's mom that got me thinking about my future.

That pivotal turning point happened one night while I was smoking dope with a group of guys in my friend's basement. His dad—a high-ranking officer with the Royal Canadian

Mounted Police who took down the notorious serial killer, Clifford Olson—offered up his basement to us as a way to keep us off the streets and out of trouble.

Midway through the evening, I headed upstairs to the kitchen for some ice and found my friend's mom sitting at the kitchen table.

"Hello, Mrs. Mortimer," I said as I headed to the freezer. "Thanks for having us at your house. How are you doing?"

Mrs. Mortimer, who worked as a registered nurse, looked at me for a long minute before speaking.

"What are you doing, Randy?" she asked finally.

I was foggy from the pot I had been smoking and was confused by her question.

"Oh, I'm just getting some ice," I replied.

Mrs. Mortimer shook her head.

"No, Randy. That's not what I'm asking. What I mean is, what are you doing with your life?"

Her words lodged in my gut but before I could come up with a response, she continued.

"Randy, you are polite and well-spoken. You are different from the others. You can do so much more with your life. Why are you hanging out with those idiots?"

I had never had an adult outside of my parents express belief in me, and her words penetrated every part of my being. Though I never finished an exam in school and was a slow reader, I knew I was smart, and I was grateful that someone of Mrs. Mortimer's caliber saw something in me. Maybe she was right. Maybe I could do something worthwhile with my life.

I had started cleaning up my act not long after that encounter, had found God and eventually landed in Bible college. But though I had escaped the life trajectory that my dad and so many of my childhood friends had followed, there was a magnetic pull inside of me that led me to serve as a volunteer prison minister as soon as I finished school. That's where I began to uncover a little more about my biological dad. Because of his criminal history, it was only a matter of time before his name came up—and when it did, inmates would approach me and ask to shake my hand.

"I partied with your dad on several occasions and he was a good man," one of the inmates told me, reiterating what others had said. "He was tough. But he had a big heart."

I hadn't thought much about my dad over the years. All I really knew of him—aside from the criminal lifestyle that had taken his life at the age of thirty-two—was that he had been a good-looking man with a chiseled jaw, five-foot-nine build, and a love of tattoos. He lived fast and hard and didn't take crap from anyone. One tattoo on his arm, which I eventually discovered while reading his autopsy report, seemed to foreshadow his life. It read veni vidi vici: I came, I saw, I conquered.

Though I knew little about him, hearing the inmates talk about my dad with such respect was like having salt rubbed into an open wound.

There was a gaping hole inside of me when it came to family. I wanted it desperately.

I began thinking more and more about my dad's side of the family. My mom had told me a little bit about his parents over the years. She told me their names, Loren and Hazel Wells, and said they lived in the BC area. But she warned that they were cold, hardened alcoholics who weren't likely to give me the connection I was craving.

"I wouldn't get your hopes up," she advised whenever the topic arose.

She also told me my dad had fathered another child, Donna, who was only a year or so younger than me.

No one on the Wells side of the family had ever reached out to me. But by the time I was thirty-one, curiosity had gotten the best of me. I decided I was going to hunt them down and try to establish a relationship.

I started with my half-sister. I searched for her name in a Criss Cross Directory and soon had a phone number.

I was so used to pain and rejection when it came to family that I didn't have much expectation. But I could still feel the hope building as I dialed the number.

I heard the phone ring. Then I heard a woman's voice.

"Hello?"

I didn't expect the emotion that such a small, innocuous word could provoke. But I knew instinctively that voice belonged to my sister.

"Is this Donna?" I asked.

"Yes, this is her."

I could hear the curiosity in her voice and it sparked a mix of anxiety and excitement inside of me.

I took a deep breath to steady myself.

"Well, I may not have the right Donna," I said, "but my name is Randall, my dad's name was Glen Wells, and I'm looking for a half-sister I've never met."

There was a pause on the other end of the phone line. When she finally spoke, her voice was a jumble of shock, disbelief, and excitement.

"I've got a brother? I can't believe it," she blurted into the phone. "No one ever told me I had a brother."

Donna and I arranged a get-together, and within a few days I was headed to Chilliwack, a town located about a forty-five-minute drive from my apartment.

Meeting Donna was like traveling back to my past. She was an attractive thirty-year-old woman with light brown hair and a medium build, whom I soon discovered ran with the same wild crowds that I did during high school.

As we talked, I learned that she had attended a neighboring

high school, had gone to several of the same parties I attended, and had even dated a buddy of mine.

Donna was pleasant and I enjoyed our conversation. But I knew we weren't going to have much of a relationship. She was a heavy drinker and smoker who seemed to be caught up in the party lifestyle I had long left behind. Aside from sharing a dad, we had little in common.

The next family members on my list were my grandparents, whom I managed to track down through Donna.

I placed a phone call to introduce myself and was soon sitting in a small apartment in Burnaby, a Vancouver suburb, taking in my dad's parents.

Loren and Hazel, now both in their seventies, were gruff, hard-drinking people who reflected years of heavy smoking. They were nice enough to me, but there was an edge to them both and I could tell they weren't people anyone would want to mess with.

Loren, a decorated World War II veteran, had spent the rest of his working life on the Vancouver docks as a longshoreman. Along with my dad, my grandparents had a son, Brian, and a daughter who died when she was four.

We didn't talk much about my dad. But Grandma Hazel did tell me how she learned of his death. "I heard it on the radio," she said, her voice still raw with pain. "They didn't give a name, but they shared the address and I knew it was Glen."

It was through newspaper clippings Donna shared with me, as well as my conversations with her and my Uncle Brian (whom I eventually connected with over the phone), that I finally learned the details surrounding my dad's murder.

According to the news reports, my dad worked as a foreman at the docks and was arrested—along with five other guys—in a $5 million heroin bust. He and the other guys were out on bail awaiting trial. But all of them were gunned down before the case could go to court.

"I saw your dad a week before he was killed," my uncle told me. "He was holed up in his house and must have suspected trouble because he had a gun on him."

Donna added the final details surrounding his death.

"He managed to place a call to 911, but the police knew his address well and were in no hurry to help," she fumed. "They stood outside smoking cigarettes before they went in."

I was numb as I took in the story surrounding my dad's death. I learned from my Uncle Brian that he always carried a picture of me in his wallet. My uncle also told me that my dad—though hard on the outside—was a softhearted guy who was known to purchase bags of groceries for people in need.

I spent a few months actively seeking out a relationship with my dad's family. But it was a one-sided effort and after a few months I moved to Calgary to pursue a better job and lost touch.

Though I didn't find the family connection I had hoped for, I did learn more about my biological dad and could definitely see some of his traits in myself. Like him, I was known to have a tough exterior, though inside I was soft and willing to do anything for anyone and give anyone the benefit of the doubt. But like my dad, I didn't put up with crap and never backed down from a fight.

I also recognized another Wells family trait, which extended to my Rush side of the family as well: my need for revenge when I had been wronged.

During my second call with my Uncle Brian, he told me about a cousin who was involved with the Mafia.

"Two years after your dad's murder, that cousin called and told me that the man who pulled the trigger had been taken care of," he said in a matter-of-fact tone.

I had worked hard to escape the life that I had been born

into and forge a new path for myself.

Though a life in the ministry had never materialized, I had pushed through the tough times with the help of my faith and managed to build a successful career—first in printing and then in sales.

I was determined to live a life I could be proud of. But I was still a kid from New Westminster, and still had the Wells/Rush family revenge DNA flowing through me.

I didn't have to know my biological dad to know how he would react if someone he cared about personally had betrayed him and conned him out of $4.6 million. And I could only imagine what my cousin would do.

Rage clawed away at my insides as I replayed the events of the launch party in my mind. Once again, I was the third-grader with the shiny Road Runner lunch box who had been pushed to the brink. Only this time, my weapon was a lot more powerful than a lunch box or a punch. Despite what they had stolen from me, I had money. Lots of it. And I was going to use it with force.

I would never do anything that broke the law or jeopardized a good night's sleep. But some of the old Randy was coming out of retirement.

Randy Rush

Above: Randy at two years and two months old, in September of 1968.

Above: Easter 1970. Randy with his first step dad Victor, along with Agnes and Billy, Victor's kids from his first marriage.

Randy Rush

Above: Randy, at age 6, driving a car for the first time.

13 Billion to One

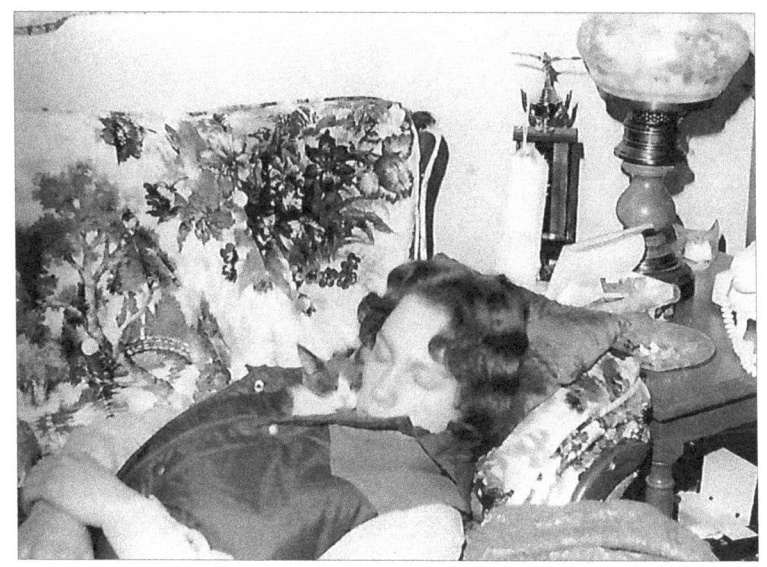

Above: Randy, at age 16, curled up with his cat, BooBoo in his vest.

Above: Randy and another family pet, cat Tommy Francesco, at age 21.

Above: Randy's biological dad, Glen Wells, then about 16 years old, with siblings Ricky and Janice.

Above: Randy's first muscle car, a 1968 SD Beaumont, in the summer of 1986.

13 Billion to One

Above: Randy towards the end of his second year of Bible school, in the spring 1987.

Randy Rush

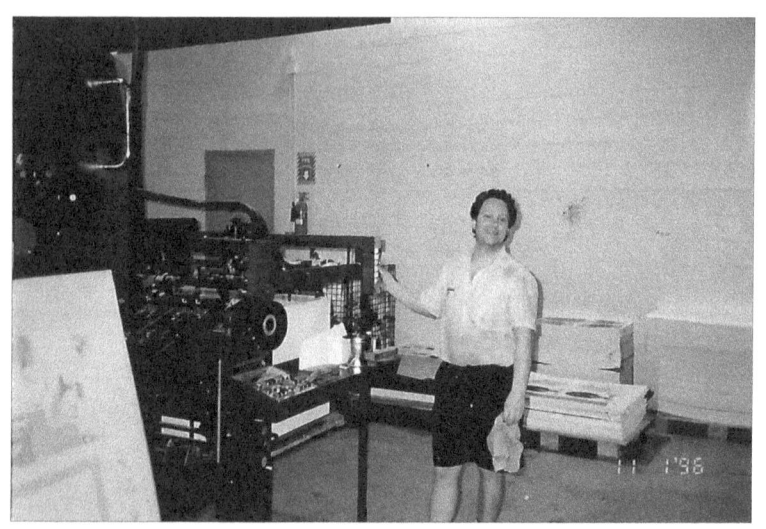

Above: Randy at age 30 working as the third pressman at Hemlock Printers. It was his first real job with health and dental benefits, which paid, after a raise, $12.43 per hour!

Above: The family's pets from the time Randy was 14 to 34. They provided many hours of laughs and entertainment, and were all good buddies.

Randy Rush

Above: Randy and his step-grandparents in the Czech Republic in 1999.

13 Billion to One

Above: Randy with his uncle Miro and Boris the dog in the Czech Republic in 1999.

Randy Rush

Above: Exterior shot of the apartment building fire that destroyed Randy's home in 2002.

13 Billion to One

Above: Inside what was left of Randy's apartment after the fire in 2002.

Randy Rush

Above: Randy and his cat, Huey, reunited after the fire. Fearing Huey had been lost in the fire, Randy was grateful to find him unharmed and hidden amongst the rubble.

Above: Randy and his friend Daryl revisiting Randy's childhood home where he lived from ages 8 to 12. Also pictured, Randy's Ferrari 458 Spyder which he affectionately called Boris, after the song by the Who.

Above: Randy holding his $50,000,000 Lotto Max check in January of 2015.

Above: Randy and Conway Kitty in 2016.

Above: Randy and Dave Crawford in Honolulu at the Canoe Club in Waikiki in April 2015, using the $25,000 Randy gave him to get him out of bankruptcy on a lavish Hawaiian vacation.

13 Billion to One

Above: Jeremy and Amy at Mama's Fish House is Maui in April 2015.

Randy Rush

Above: A painting of Conway Kitty commissioned by Randy by Madison van der Gulik.

Above: A house Randy bought in the Ottawa area as investment. He let his friends Brent and Kim Lackie and their three kids live there free of charge, covering all maintenance, mortgage and insurance payments.

Above: Randy with former Canadian Prime Minister Jean Chrétien, who he met as a result of his lottery win.

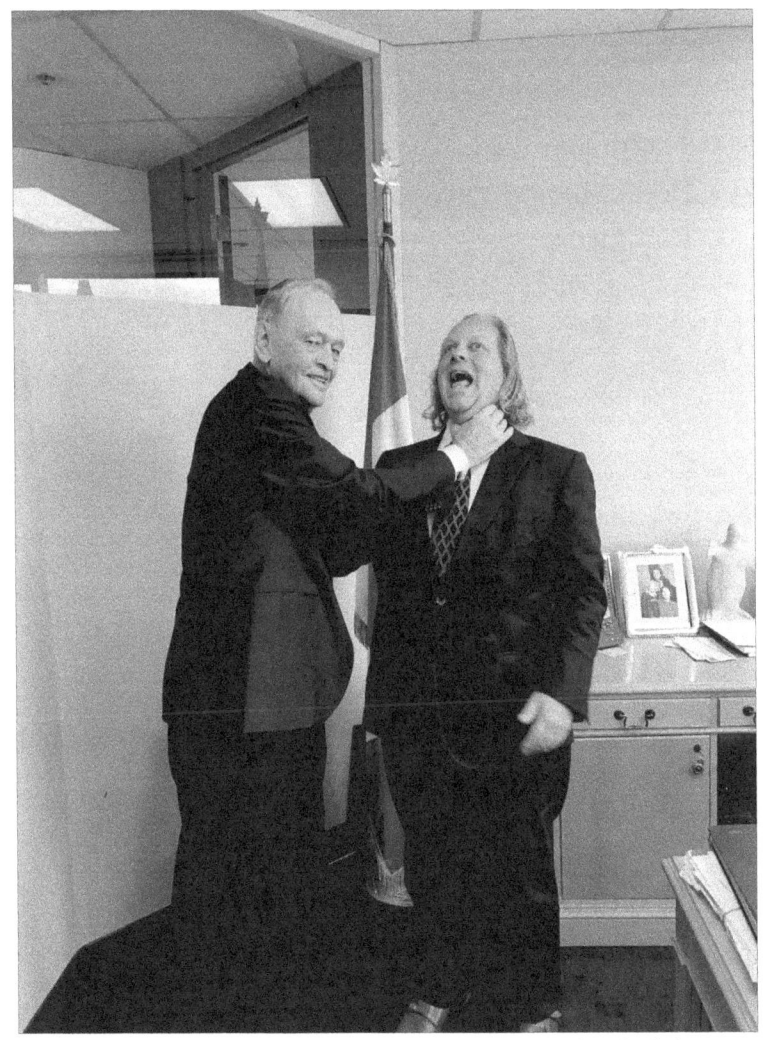

Above: Former Canadian Prime Minister Jean Chrétien greeting Randy with a " Shawinigan handshake," in reference to a 1996 incident in which Chrétien choked a protester to the ground.

Above: Randy and Daryl (with a golden eagle perched on his head) at St. Andrews in 2015. Daryl was one of Randy's closest friends for over 20 years, and one of those who helped him the most after the 2002 apartment fire. He passed away in March of 2019.

Above: Early development of the KULTiD app, taken in Scottsdale, AZ in May 2015.

Above: KULTiD launch party tickets, on November 1, 2015. Photo used by permission of Aaron Scolfield.

13 Billion to One

Above: The Scottsdale, AZ property Randy recovered after winning litigation against Jeremy in 2016. Not including his 1957 Corvette (pictured).

Above: Randy and Coco the parrot, reunited in 2007 after his bird-napping.

Above: Randy with the students of a primary school he supports in Kenya in February 2017.

15

I was ready to do whatever it took to get my money back and exact some revenge. And I knew it started with hiring the best attorney I could find.

As much as the thought infuriated me, my gut was telling me the $2 million I had turned over for operating expenses was gone. I wasn't even sure what recourse I had when it came to the hard assets, given that Jeremy had put his and Amy's names on the property titles. But when my team and I had finished giving statements to the attorneys at Snell and Wilmer, one of Arizona's top law firms, I was assured I had a strong case. I was also assured that the litigation wouldn't be cheap.

"I'm pretty sure we can get your hard assets back," the attorney told me. "But it's going to cost you around $200,000."

It was hard to grasp that this was the world I was now living in. Nine months earlier, $200,000 would have represented an entire year's salary for me. I would have laughed out loud if someone had told me I would be shelling that out in attorney fees. But now it didn't even faze me. My mind quickly ran through the calculations: Spend $200,000 to get back nearly $2 million in assets.

I could see Jeremy's sneer and hear his words from the launch party ripping through my mind: *I own everything. You have nothing.*

He had followed that up with an email the next morning telling me that we were finished and that I was no longer invited to invest in KULT Labs. There was no mention of the millions of dollars I had put in. Just a severing of ties. I was furious. I was sitting on a pile of cash and was willing to spend $2 million going after him if it meant taking him down.

"That's fine," I replied to the attorney. "Let's do it."

Our strategy was to start with a civil lawsuit against Jeremy, Amy, and Ross Richardson, suing them for fourteen claims, including fraud. I had originally been unclear of Ross's role in all of this. But as Mike and Max began reviewing the pro forma that Ross had provided a few days earlier and asking him basic questions about finances, it became clear that he either didn't know what he was talking about or was stonewalling us.

"This is a joke," Max fumed after reviewing the financial document. "It looks like something a twelfth grader would put together for a class project."

Despite his behavior leading up to the launch party, I had been hesitant to lump Ross in with Jeremy because of his position as a church pastor. It was hard for me to reconcile that a man who held himself out as a servant of God would purposely help con me out of millions of dollars.

But Ross ignored requests for information from Mike in the days following the launch party, and as I continued talks with my attorney, it became clear that Jeremy could never have pulled off the theft without him. Max and Mike were in full agreement.

"He was the one holding the purse strings," Max stressed.

"The money wouldn't have gone out the door if he hadn't allowed it to happen."

I headed to the Mexican Riviera with Brent and Mike for a preplanned getaway while the attorneys at Snell and Wilmer began working on the lawsuit. But it was impossible to get into vacation mode. I had been so high on the KULTiD software and its game-changing potential that I was struggling to wrap my mind around the notion that the company was mostly a front to steal money from me. I was seething with rage, but it wasn't just Jeremy and crew fueling the fire. I was so angry with myself I could barely stand to look in the mirror. There had been so many warning signs, but I had been so caught up in the excitement I had ignored them all.

How could I have been such an idiot? I had been visualizing my lottery win for years and had spent countless hours planning out how I would conduct my affairs so I could avoid being taken. I knew lottery winners were easy targets and I thought I had surrounded myself with good people who had my back. Instead, I had brought the wolf into my house—literally.

The idea that Dave could serve me up to his son and then stand by and watch him sink his teeth into me was so painful it was like having a knife jammed into my gut and twisted every time I thought of him.

Even though my head and gut were screaming otherwise, a piece of my heart had initially still held out hope that maybe Dave was just an innocent bystander who had naively told his son about my good fortune and handed over my number. I knew Shirley had played a pivotal role in the title fraud involving the Sherwood Park home by placing it in Jeremy and Amy's name, but it was so hard to fathom that the people I loved so much and had done so much for would turn on me that I had downplayed her betrayal in my mind.

Dave protested my initial text demanding that he leave

my house, arguing that he and Shirley weren't involved and shouldn't be punished. At first, I had actually felt bad about it and wondered if I was being too hard on him. But when I reiterated that his son had just taken me for nearly $5 million, Dave didn't express even a shred of concern for me. All he cared about was losing his gravy train.

"Well, I hope the two of you can work things out," he replied. "It's between the two of you. Don't throw us under the bus."

My mind flashed to that late August evening in the kitchen of my log-cabin house, when Dave put his arm around my shoulder and joined Shirley in assuring me that I had nothing to worry about with their son.

My fingers were on fire as I pounded out my text to him.

"There's nothing to work out. We are through and you better be out of my house by the time I get back to Canada. If you're not, I'll throw you out myself."

❖

Jeremy and I were engaged in a game of chess. And I knew that if I didn't play it right, he was going to corner my king before I got to his.

We had filed the lawsuit and served Jeremy and Ross with the papers on November 17, which I gleefully discovered was Amy's birthday. But Jeremy had also made a bold play, helping Dave and Shirley move into my Sherwood Park house. When I got word of it from Lisa, I lost my nuts.

"Get out of my house now or pay my rent or I'm suing you!" I demanded.

I could almost hear Dave's laugh in his response.

"We don't owe you anything. This is Jeremy and Amy's house and we are here as invited guests."

The fire inside of me was so intense it was blocking my airways. It was almost as though Jeremy and Shirley had planned this out in advance. But until I battled it out in court, I knew that I was stuck.

"Leave it alone for now, Randy," my friends advised. "You've got bigger rocks to overturn right now."

I knew they were right. Jeremy was the boulder in all of this and I had to get him removed before it was too late. As long as he was living in my Scottsdale house, had his name on the property titles, and still had access to KULT Lab bank accounts, I knew I was in serious trouble.

After spending eight months ignoring my intuition, I was now paying close attention to gut instinct. And what it was telling me was that I wasn't Jeremy's first victim.

While pacing my hotel room in Mexico, I remembered a casual comment Jeremy had made a few months earlier while we were palling around in Edmonton. He had taken me to meet Ernie, a guy who ran a local dealership, and, after leaving, he mentioned that Ernie had invested a few dollars in KULTiD.

I didn't think much of it at the time because I knew that for all practical purposes, I was the only investor. But now it set off an alarm.

"I'll bet I'm not the only one," I announced to Mike and Brent over breakfast the next morning. "I'll bet he's done this before."

I hired a private investigator to start looking into Jeremy's background, and then I kicked off my own investigation by placing a call to Ernie.

"Everything has blown up and gone to hell with KULTiD," I told him as soon as I had him on the phone. "I've lost millions and remembered Jeremy saying you put in some money as well. Is that true?"

Ernie was silent for a minute.

"Yeah, I invested in it," he said finally. "I put in $30,000, and a couple of the guys who work here put in some money as well. We all lost our shirts."

"You should talk with Jim," he added. "I think he put in some money, too. Jeremy's been at this for a while."

His words seeped into my gut and I could feel the knot forming. Jim had invested, too? I knew he was a KULT Labs employee. I had no idea he was also an investor. Though I knew Jeremy had been working on the software concept for a while, he had presented KULTiD as a new ground-floor proposition. Instead, it sounded like he had been dangling it as a carrot to steal people's money for years.

My thoughts jumped to the mid-September email I had received from Jeremy asking for another million-dollar infusion and the nonstop pressure he had applied the week leading up to the launch party. I could hear his sobs as he pleaded for more funding, and I could see the ridiculous proposal to use the property I had already purchased as collateral for the new loan.

Panic shot through me as the realization hit.

"He's out of money and is going to liquidate my assets," I blurted to Mike. "If we don't stop him, everything's going to be gone."

I was a volcano ready to erupt as I relayed my concerns to Bill Klain, an Arizona attorney who had just taken over our case after Snell and Wilmer realized they had done some intellectual property work for KULT Labs and couldn't represent me.

The team at Snell and Wilmer had tried unsuccessfully to get my assets frozen without providing prior notice to Jeremy when they took on the case in early November. Bill tried it again—citing the company's lack of cash, our growing concerns, the blatant title fraud committed by Jeremy, and the mounting evidence suggesting a pattern of fraud. To overcome the judge's initial ruling, Bill's motion also stipulated that Jeremy would receive prior notice of the temporary restraining order.

This strategy worked.

On November 25, the day before American Thanksgiving, Judge Whitten approved our request and the temporary restraining order (TRO) went into immediate effect. It listed the office building, the Scottsdale house, the Sherwood Park house, and the Audi R8—all of the assets I had purchased as part of my original collateral agreement with Jeremy. It also included all of the vehicles Jeremy had purchased since June, and prevented Jeremy from encumbering the assets in any way. In addition, it stopped Jeremy from transferring any money from his personal or KULT Lab accounts within the US to any accounts outside of the country.

At least for the moment, I was a move ahead.

16

WAS RELIEVED THAT MY ASSETS were at least temporarily safeguarded. But I knew I needed more documentation of Jeremy's frauds if I was going to nail him and keep my assets frozen until I could get them back.

"What we need is someone on the inside," I noted to Mike as we caught a flight to Arizona the following week to meet with Bill and devise a game plan. "We need a mole."

A magic genie must have been listening in on our conversation because what happened next was nothing short of miraculous.

After we wrapped up our meeting with Bill on Friday afternoon, he had swung by Safeway to pick up a few groceries for dinner. That's where he ran into Jason, an old acquaintance he hadn't seen for nearly fifteen years. While catching up, Jason mentioned that he had just been laid off from a software app company that had run into problems.

"I can't talk with you until you have spoken to an attorney," Bill responded as soon as he learned that the company was

KULT Labs. "I'm representing Randy Rush."

Jason, according to Bill, immediately became animated and told him that he and other ex-employees had been wanting to talk with me for several weeks.

"You're kidding me!" I exclaimed when Bill shared the news and told me I would soon be hearing from Jason. "This is incredible."

By the time I spoke with Jason later that evening, he had already contacted Aaron, another former KULT employee, who was also anxious to talk with me. They both offered to meet with Mike and me separately the next day for taped interviews.

I knew I needed to hear what the two men had to say because I suspected that they held vital inside information that would bolster my court case.

But I would have never guessed that the two former employees had been conned by Jeremy as well.

I had met Jason and Aaron on several occasions while visiting the KULT offices. They were the two marketing executives Jeremy had told me he wanted to bring on when he hit me up for the $2 million operating capital in mid-June. I had assumed he had found them through a headhunter or a job posting. Instead, it sounded like he used my money—specifically money he had pressured me into putting up for the luxury swimming pool and Audi R8—as bait to ensnare them.

The men's stories were so similar it was like listening to a rerun of a bad movie—one that I had inadvertently funded.

They both stressed that they were happily employed in stable jobs when Jeremy showed up waving a wad of cash. Jason told me he met him when the swimming pool company he worked for was hired to install the high-end pool at the Scottsdale house I financed as part of my collateral agreement. Aaron, a sales rep at a nearby Audi dealership, said he encountered Jeremy when he walked in and slapped down $120,000 in cash for the fully-loaded Audi R8 he had badgered me into funding.

"You see that sometimes, but it's impressive," Aaron admitted.

After dazzling them with his mirage of wealth, the men said that Jeremy had dangled big money jobs at KULT Labs that he guaranteed would make them millionaires within three years. In each case, Jeremy invited them to stop by the KULT offices, where, like me, the men said they were wowed by the hip work space, the slick PowerPoint presentation, and—above all—Ross Richardson.

Listening to Aaron describe his first impression of Ross was so identical to mine it was like reliving the experience all over again.

"Here's this guy who I was told had just sold a company for $77 million and was a pastor at the CCV church, a really well-known church in Phoenix," Aaron noted. "That someone of his caliber was going to be the CFO of the company really said something to me.

"What really caught my attention was that Jeremy said Forbes had done a projection on his company and estimated that it would be worth $20 to $30 billion in three to five years," Aaron added.

His words came at me like a swarm of wasps. Where was the line for that low-life? Wasn't it enough that he had conned the money out of me? Did he really have to use it to screw over others as well?

I bit my lip to keep from screaming and forced my face to stay neutral as the two men continued with their accounts.

After confirming with Jeremy that he owned patents on the app, and that the company was flush with cash reserves thanks to the "forty investors" Jeremy assured them were backing the company, both men said they jumped at the opportunity to earn the seven-figure salaries that Jeremy promised would eventually be theirs. But they told me their joy was short-lived.

According to Jason, the nagging concerns started for him at the company kickoff summit in late July, when he noticed that everything appeared disorganized and out of control. He said it was a concern that intensified as things went on and he realized no one was manning the ship.

"Jeremy was rarely in the office," Jason explained. "Out of the five months I was there, I would say he was in the office for a month of that—leaving us without any direction."

His words lodged in my gut. Just a couple of months earlier, I had discovered that Jeremy was paying himself nearly $30,000 a month. I also learned that he was paying Amy $12,000 a month to handle social media—which both Jason and Aaron told me was essentially nonexistent. The salaries had seemed excessive for a start-up, but when I raised it with Jeremy, he shrugged me off.

"If you want quality, you've got to pay for it," he replied.

As the men continued to share their experiences at KULT, their accounts turned to Jeremy's reckless, irresponsible spending, confirming everything I had suspected and had come to discover myself: the hundreds of thousands of dollars spent on luxury sports cars, the tens of thousands of dollars spent on season tickets to sporting events, and the extreme waste on needless office remodels and expensive workstations. But what I didn't know was how much Jeremy purposely impeded the success of the app.

As sales and marketing executives, the men said they had been tasked with bringing on brands to the app. But when they asked for tools to do their job, they said they were shut down.

"We asked if we could purchase premiere LinkedIn accounts so that we could contact decision-makers directly," Aaron explained. "The premiere accounts cost $800 each, but they're worthwhile because you get direct email access. But we were told there was no money for that. Then, the very next day, Jeremy buys a $4,000 espresso machine so he can have his daily espresso without having to cross the street to Starbucks."

I could feel my fingernails digging into my palms as I took in that piece of information. I had seen Jeremy use it to steam his milk and prepare a shot of espresso. It had seemed a little extravagant but I had no idea he had wasted $4,000 of my money on that. Had I known that he was pulling that kind of crap while blocking much-needed funds for marketing, I would have dropped that machine on his head.

Aaron told me they had continued to plead for marketing support—such as advertising on Facebook or securing a booth at the Phoenix fashion show that was being attended by all the big apparel brands—but were denied. And even after managing to secure contracts, the men said there were no procedures in place to load the brands onto the app and train them on how the app worked.

On top of it all, the men told me they discovered right before the launch party that they had been selling lies to the brands they contacted.

"Jeremy had told us there were 100,000 preregistered users," Jason recalled bitterly. "But we found out that there were actually only 650 of them—and they had all come from our efforts on Facebook in the three and a half months prior to the launch."

The revelations slammed into me like a sledgehammer. Peddling those kinds of lies to brands was not only unethical, it was business suicide. How did Jeremy think he was going to get away with that? And how was it possible that there was no actual procedure to get brands and their merchandise set up on the app? Brand partnerships were the entire point of it.

My head was pounding so hard it felt like it was going to explode. But I forced myself to breathe and keep going with the interviews.

In each of their accounts, the men described a demoralized, disorganized workplace environment. They said Ross, who they claimed was only in the office about fifty percent of the time, had no control over the finances and missed direct deposit payroll twice.

"When Ross was in the office, he spent much of his time working on Jeremy's personal finances and helping him with his immigration status," Jason noted. "And after the launch party, he stopped coming in altogether."

It took everything I could do to keep my cool. Ross was being paid $200,000 a year to guide the company financially and instead had spent his time screwing around or serving as Jeremy's accomplice.

I didn't think it could get any worse than what I now knew. But Jason wasn't done. He told me that when Jeremy wasn't traveling between Canada and Arizona working on his immigration status, he spent a lot of his time vacationing in California and liked it so much that he had recently bought a home on the beach.

It was like I'd just had a dump truck of wet cement poured on me. I'd known that Jeremy had used my money to finance luxury cars and a lavish lifestyle. But the idea that he had used the operating capital I had put up for KULTiD to fund an ocean getaway in California was more than I could stomach. My legs were shaking under the table and I could feel the veins bulging in my neck.

"He purchased a house?" I managed, fighting to keep my voice under control. "Do you know where it is?"

Jason nodded. "It's in Oceanside—a lease-to-own property. It's a brand-new unit right on the water.

"I have pictures if you want to see them," he added.

The men wrapped up their stories by telling me that after

a direct deposit paycheck was missed for a second time on November 20, Michael DeRaffel, the new COO they said Jeremy had met at church in California, called a staff meeting and told everyone it was unclear how much longer they could keep the company afloat. And on November 30, Jason, Aaron, and a few other employees were laid off—not by Jeremy, who was off on vacation, or Ross, who was nowhere to be found—but by Michael.

Their accounts made my stomach cramp. During their interviews, both men told me they had expressed serious reservations over the launch party—both because they thought it was a waste of resources, and because they knew the app wasn't ready and still had bugs to work out. On top of that, they said they were concerned that the Android version wasn't ready, which, as Trevor had pointed out at the launch party, meant that nearly seventy percent of potential customers wouldn't even be able to access it.

As the magnitude of Jeremy's greed and deception and Ross's complicit role continued to sink in, my mind replayed the monthly visits I had made to Arizona in the four months leading up to the launch party. I could see Jeremy as he spewed his continual lies about the skyrocketing valuation of KULT Labs and the through-the-roof excitement that KULTiD was generating among the high-powered brand partners who were coming on board. I could also hear the buzz of energy that I had experienced—or at least thought I had experienced—whenever I stopped by the office. Clearly it was all a show. Now, there was only one question screaming for an answer.

"You could see all these things going on," I said to Jason, no longer able to hide my anger and frustration. "Why wasn't I contacted?"

Jason shook his head.

"We were told you were a silent investor. I had no idea that you wanted interaction."

My blood vessels felt like they were going to pop. I didn't think I could take any more, but Jason still wasn't through.

"When we had the party at the hockey game, I asked 'Where's Randy?' Jeremy said, 'This is not for investors. They will sit down there on the ice. Not up with us.'

"And while we were there, Jeremy's mom came up to my girlfriend and me and said, 'I have a new two-door Mercedes and I really like it.' She thought she was the sh#!. We didn't even know how to respond to that."

Each disclosure by Jason and Aaron was like peeling back another layer of an onion. And some of them generated their own bitter aha moments in my mind as I correlated their information with bits of information I had been gathering.

I didn't know the full story behind the Mercedes now in Shirley's possession. But I knew it was the same Mercedes Jeremy had been driving when I first met him. I had recently learned that $150,000 was an outrageous sum of money to pay for the development of a mobile phone app, and I suspected that Jeremy had used some of that initial seed money to purchase the car.

I could taste the bitterness surging through me. My mind locked on the barrage of phone calls I had received from Jeremy only weeks after hitting the lottery jackpot. The Crawfords had played me so completely.

I was still supposed to be soaking in the wonder of the tremendous gift I had been given. I should have still been high on the euphoria of it all. I should have been relaxing in a villa in Greece or just continuing the celebration with my friends.

Jeremy hadn't just taken my money. He had stolen my joy.

My thoughts turned from my personal circumstances to those of Jason and Aaron's. Both men had confided that they had been living paycheck to paycheck since joining KULT Labs and were now broke and jobless three weeks before Christmas because they had put their trust in Jeremy.

I didn't know just how pervasive Jeremy's cons were, but it was clear that numerous people had already been financially and emotionally devastated by him.

The anger that had been fueling me for the past month was settling into a steely resolve. I was going to get justice—not just for me, but for Jason and Aaron and everyone else who had been hurt by Jeremy and any other Crawford.

"Listen, I'm going to cover your salaries for a couple of months so you can get back on your feet," I told the men after wrapping up my interviews with each of them.

"And I'm making a promise right now," I added, reiterating a vow that I had made several times since the launch party. "I'm putting an end to Jeremy's scams. He's not going to hurt anyone else and he's going to pay for what he's done. I'm taking this scumbag down."

17

It was like someone had thrown a stick of lighted dynamite into the quicksand that was once again consuming me. This time it was Drew Porter, the head app designer at KULT Labs, who struck the match.

"Randy, Jeremy is taking out a mortgage on your house," he announced the second I answered my phone.

His words ignited a rage inside of me. I knew he was wrong, that what he was saying was impossible. But I was so unnerved that I was shaking, and my legs felt like they were about to buckle underneath me.

"Drew, he can't!" I heard myself boom into the phone. "There's a restraining order. The assets are frozen."

It was Thursday, December 10, only two weeks into the temporary restraining order, and just five days since Jason and Aaron had put me in touch with Drew.

Drew was still employed and had agreed to be my inside eyes and ears—even though it meant putting his job at risk. I don't know what I was expecting from him. Maybe an occasional report about the inner workings of the company. Certainly not this.

I inhaled and waited for Drew to respond, to tell me that his phone call was all a sick practical joke. But when he spoke again, he only cemented the nightmare.

"I'm just telling you what's happening," he said in a firm, quiet tone. "I thought you would want to know."

The blood must have drained from my head because I was suddenly so light-headed I couldn't stand. I collapsed into a chair in my room at the W Hotel, struggling to fight back the waves of panic crashing over me. It didn't matter that a judge had barred Jeremy from liquidating my assets. I knew deep down he had found a way.

Jeremy was a snake that slithered around the law and found the cracks. He had already managed to liquidate the Audi R8 and the 1999 Ferrari Spider by trading them in for a much less expensive Porsche 911 and $125,000 in cash. He had pulled off the theft on November 23, just two days before the TRO hearing he knew was coming.

When Bill notified me of the car liquidations that he had just learned about from Jeremy's attorney, Andre Merrett, I was so livid it took every internal restraint I had to keep from hunting Jeremy down and kicking in his teeth. Mike, who had been by my side since the launch party, did his best to hold me together.

"At least he can't do anything else, Randy," he'd said, reiterating a similar statement from Bill. "His hands are tied now. We've got him and the rest will be worked out in court."

I had hung on to those words for the past week, trying to convince myself that my remaining assets were safe. But now I knew otherwise.

I hung up with Drew and placed a frantic call to Bill. He, in turn, contacted Andre, who assured him that I had received false information and there was nothing to worry about.

I didn't care what Jeremy's attorney said. My gut was telling me that Jeremy was up to no good and I was done with thinking that he would play by the rules.

"I don't know how he's doing it, but he's doing it," I ranted to anyone who would listen. "And we've got to get to the bottom of it and stop him."

At my urging, Bill's team began conducting public record searches on the County Recorder's website. The tip from Drew and Bill's subsequent call to Andre Merrett must have stopped Jeremy from trying to liquidate the equity in my house. But within a few days, Bill's team uncovered another nightmare: Jeremy had managed to take out a $200,000 mortgage on my office building.

"This is illegal!" I screamed when I heard the news. "How can this happen? There is a restraining order in place."

The explanation was one I dreaded but deep down expected: Jeremy had once again managed to slither through the cracks. Between the Thanksgiving holiday weekend and the general processing time required, the lien that Bill had filed on the properties hadn't made it into the system. As such, when Jeremy went in to sign the paperwork, the title to the property came up clear. And because his name was on the title and no money was owed on it, the mortgage company assumed he was legitimate.

Bill, who was as outraged as I was by Jeremy's blatant lies and disregard for the law, whipped off an angry email to Andre. "Your client lied to you," he fumed. "He took out a $200,000 mortgage on the office building and is now in contempt. We are going to court!"

My emotions swung by the minute. Sometimes I was so consumed by rage I wanted to destroy anything in my path. Other times, I was so full of despair it was a struggle to pull myself out of bed. I spent hours staring at the ceiling in my hotel room, replaying the last eight months over and over in my mind. What I couldn't shake was that it was my devotion to my faith and belief that Dave, Jeremy, and Ross were committed Christians that had gotten me into this mess. They had all called me "brother," an endearing term used among church members, and had often referred to their prayers and guidance from God—playing on my spiritual beliefs to screw me out of a tenth of my lottery winnings.

A fresh rush of rage shot through me every time I thought of Dave putting his arm around my shoulder and assuring me that I had nothing to worry about with Jeremy, followed by Shirley's assurance that I was in good hands because Jeremy was a good Christian. The final kick in the gut was Ross Richardson's role in it all. They had to have known that his being a pastor would carry a lot of weight with me.

Bill secured an emergency hearing on December 17. It didn't take much to convince Judge Whitten, who had issued the temporary restraining order, to enter an order demanding that Jeremy return the $200,000 to the court no later than five p.m. on December 21 or be in contempt and face stiff fines. On Bill's request, the judge also ordered Jeremy to turn over all company records and bank account information for himself and for KULT Labs.

It was a victory, but I was having a hard time celebrating. All I could think about was the millions of dollars that had been stolen from me and the long legal battle that I knew was ahead.

I spent most of the next four days pacing my hotel room, thinking about the December 21 deadline and wondering if my $200,000 would be there. I wanted to believe that Jeremy would follow the law, but I couldn't shake the doubts and sinking feeling that now gripped me. Between my ongoing digging and the private investigator I had hired, I was piecing together a detailed picture of Jeremy's ongoing con. Through bits of information provided by Drew, Jason, and Aaron and my own trolling of Jeremy's Facebook page, I was able to prove that on the day Jason, Aaron, and other employees were laid off due to lack of funds, Jeremy and his family were living it up in California on my dime. Using photos of the Oceanside condo Jason had provided and sale searches in the area, I was also able to pinpoint the address for the lease-to-own condo Jeremy had acquired with $80,000 from KULT Labs.

I was fixated on getting my money back and making Jeremy pay. But the more I learned, the more I feared that he would get away with it. My private investigator had reported that Amy was back in Canada and to me this meant one thing: that Jeremy was likely moving my money across the border and getting ready to flee the country.

Every new revelation was another slap in the face and I could taste the bitterness as I thought about Dave and Shirley squatting in my house in Canada while Jeremy and his family continued to occupy my house in Arizona, living high on the hog on my money. It was more than my brain could process and I didn't know how much longer I could take it.

The December 21 deadline came and went without any action by Jeremy. And when we headed back to court on December 22, it was clear Judge Whitten was done playing games.

Like the week before, Jeremy wasn't in attendance at the hearing. And when Andre Merrett tried to explain away his client's lack of compliance by saying he didn't have the money to turn over and shouldn't be punished for being broke, Judge Whitten wasn't hearing it.

"That's not why he's being punished," Judge Whitten snapped. "He's going to be punished for taking it out in violation—in knowing violation—of the court's order and not replacing it."

The judge slapped Jeremy with a $10,000 a day fine until he returned the $200,000, blocked him from encumbering the Oceanside condo in any way, and prohibited him from spending any more of the $125,000 in proceeds he had received from the sale of the Audi and Ferrari. He also ordered that both the Cayenne Turbo and Porsche 911 Jeremy had recently acquired be delivered to a luxury car dealership we had secured for storage and protection.

I sat in the back of the courtroom with Mike, taking in the judge's words. I was relieved that he was coming down hard on Jeremy. But I was so emotionally drained that it was hard to get excited. Jeremy had proven that he didn't care about laws or judgments so I wasn't sure what good Judge Whitten's orders would do.

The proceedings were wrapping up when Andre stepped up to address the judge.

"I just want to give you a heads up and Mr. Klain a heads up that very shortly you should be receiving from me either a motion to withdraw with client consent or a motion without."

I was stunned. Jeremy's attorney was quitting?

I knew Andre had been repeatedly lied to by Jeremy and that he had been publicly embarrassed in court by Bill, who had proven several times that Jeremy had deceived him. But even so, I knew it was nearly unheard of for an attorney to walk away from a client.

My mood did a sudden one-eighty. If Jeremy's own attorney had decided he had enough, maybe there was a light at the end of this tunnel.

I held a straight face until I was out of the courtroom. Then I let loose.

"Sweet!" I shouted, high-fiving Mike. "Jeremy is going down."

❖

Christmas music pumped through the W Hotel, and elaborate lights and holiday decorations filled the lobby and guest areas. It was a fun, festive atmosphere—or at least it should have been. But no matter how hard I tried, I couldn't stave off the lump and darkness inside.

It was another Christmas holiday and I was alone—holed up in a fancy hotel in Arizona. I had a pile of money, several houses, and a boatload of fancy cars, but I had no one to share it with. I loved Conway Kitty, and I'd been visiting him whenever I needed a break from the KULTiD fiasco, but I yearned for human connection.

Mike had flown home to be with his family after the hearing, but I had stayed on because I had nowhere else to go.

I tried to shake the loneliness that engulfed me as I thought about all of my friends, enjoying the holidays with their spouses and kids. All I had were my parents, who were living in the Czech Republic. But I would have steered clear of them even if they were in town and staying in the room adjacent to me, because our only Christmas tradition was a family fight.

I don't know what caused it, but every Christmas we spent together ended up in some sort of an explosion. When I worked at Jasper Printing in my early thirties, we had a running contest to see which family erupted in the worst holiday fight. I won it three of the four years I was there. It was like a running joke, except that it wasn't funny.

The last time I celebrated Christmas with my mom was eleven years earlier. She had moved into my Edmonton apartment the month before because she was applying for residency in the Czech Republic and needed to be in Canada while the paperwork was being processed.

Christmas morning had started off well enough. I kissed my mom on the cheek as soon as she walked into the living room, wished her a Merry Christmas, and then set to work ironing my Sunday clothes for a church service we planned to attend.

I had just finished when my cat, Huey, began meowing for food. Without giving it another thought, I grabbed his food bowl and dumped his water down the kitchen sink drain so I could fill it with fresh water and the special gourmet canned food I had purchased for the holiday.

That's when my mom came unglued.

"Are you out of your mind?" she screamed. "Are you stupid? That's where I'm putting my turkey."

Her words came at me like a knife. It was always like this with her. Some small thing would set her off and she would berate me. Only I was no longer a little kid who could be punished at whim. I was a thirty-eight-year-old man who had been kind enough to let her stay with me. Besides that, I had done nothing wrong. It wasn't like I had filled the sink with used cat litter. It was water—and I had poured it directly over the drain. It hadn't even touched the sink.

My body tensed as I turned to face her.

"Yeah," I replied, fighting to keep my voice calm, "but I was planning to clean the sink with bleach before you put the turkey in anyway.

"It's Christmas morning," I added. "Can we talk about this later?"

Mom was Irish through and through with a fiery tempter that matched her auburn red hair. Though she was only five foot two, she had an oversized need to be right and never backed down from an argument.

"No! We are talking about it NOW."

I wanted to keep the peace. But something inside of me snapped. I grabbed the iron and threw it at a wall across the room. Then I picked up the ironing board and threw that, too.

"Merry Christmas!" I yelled.

Somewhere in the chaos that ensued, I heard my mom shouting that I could have hit her and ordering me to leave.

I grabbed my jacket and wallet and stormed out of my apartment into the frigid winter weather. There were three hotels in a four-block radius and I headed toward them, figuring I could check in for a day or two. But every place I checked was full.

I spent a few minutes walking aimlessly in the -38°C weather until I found a bench in a deserted Safeway parking lot.

My face and hands stung from the cold. But it was nothing compared to the stinging inside of me. *What was wrong with my family? Why couldn't we have one peaceful, enjoyable holiday?*

As I hugged my body in an effort to stay warm, an image of another Christmas nightmare filled my mind. I was thirty-three and had suggested that we spend the holiday in the Czech Republic with my dad's family. I loved to travel and was in the mood for an adventure. I also had friends who lived in another part of the country and I planned to visit them while there.

Everything was going well until Christmas Eve rolled around. A family friend living in the next village had invited us to a traditional Christmas Eve party at his house and I had been looking forward to the event all day. My parents had seemed excited about it as well. But a few minutes before we were set to leave, my mom announced that she didn't feel like going.

"You and Steve go without me," she said, heading to her bedroom.

I was disappointed but determined not to let her decision impact my Christmas Eve. My stepdad said he would be ready to go in an hour. I knew the party was getting underway and I didn't want to miss out. But I swallowed my frustration.

An hour passed. Then another half-hour. I finally had

enough.

"Come on, it's time to get going," I said, standing up to leave.

My stepdad didn't move from his chair.

"I don't feel like going."

The clamps tightened around my gut. He knew how much I wanted to go to this party. They both did. I didn't necessarily want to go alone. But I wasn't going to let them cheat me out of a nice Christmas Eve.

"Okay, can I have the keys?" I replied, heading toward the door. "I'm going."

My reaction must have caught Steve off guard because for a few seconds, he didn't say or do anything. Then he shook his head. "You can't take the car. You aren't on the registration."

It was as though he had reached inside me and pulled the trigger. Was this some sick joke? They knew I needed a car. We had discussed this in-depth and they had talked me out of renting one, saying it was unnecessary because we could all share.

"What do you mean I'm not on the registration? You told me I was. We talked about this."

Steve shot me a defiant look. "Your mom forgot to do it."

This was it. I was done with their manipulative control games. I wasn't a teenager anymore. I was a thirty-three-year-old man who was going to drive to the next village to celebrate a traditional Czech Christmas Eve. And in two days, I was going to drive the 125 miles to visit my friends. And they weren't going to stop me.

"I'm going," I said, my voice quiet but firm. "GIVE me the keys."

Steve couldn't beat me into submission like he did when I was young. But he wasn't about to back down.

"What are you going to do about it if I don't?"

The memory of that night was so vivid and raw it hurt just thinking about it. I never did make it to the Christmas Eve party. Like every other Christmas, my parents had managed to ruin it for me.

A cocktail of rage, hurt, and sadness swirled through me as the most recent holiday disaster replayed in my mind. I wasn't proud of the way I had exploded, taking out my anger on the iron and the wall. But I couldn't take it anymore.

I don't know how long I sat on that bench in the Safeway parking lot. But by the time my nearly frostbitten nose told me it was time to get going and find a friend I could crash with for a day or two, there was only one thought repeating in my mind: "This is the last Christmas I'm spending with my family. I'm done."

The bustle of excited chatter and laughter brought me back to the lounge at the W Hotel. It was two days before Christmas and suddenly I didn't want to be alone. A couple of days earlier, my attorney, Bill, had invited me to spend Christmas with his family. I had declined at the time, not wanting to put him or his family out. But he had persisted, stressing that they would love to have me and that it would be a lot of fun. I knew it's what I wanted.

I contacted Bill to let him know I was in, and on Christmas Eve, I found myself in a festive, love-filled home with a small gathering of Bill's friends and family, enjoying great food, company, and conversation. Bill's wife and two young daughters greeted me with open arms, and they all surprised me with a Christmas gift: an Arizona Cardinals jersey.

I enjoyed all of the guests. But I was particularly drawn to Bill's close friend, Peter Swann, an Arizona Court of Appeals Judge.

Peter was fun and full of crazy, off-the-wall stories that I would never have associated with a high-level judge. He told me that as a teenager in the 1980s, he had formed a punk rock band with the now-famous film actor Ben Stiller called Capital Punishment that had even self-released an album called *Roadkill*. That album, explained Peter, had been found by a company called Captured Tracks—which had recently rereleased it. To everyone's surprise, he said the punk rock album was gaining a huge following in Kazakhstan.

I was rolling with laughter as Peter described his sudden ascent to punk rock stardom in the obscure, far-off country. But that wasn't Peter's only crazy story.

"Tell him your John Lennon story," Bill urged.

Hearing the name of one of my musical idols got my full attention.

Maybe it was my obsession with the Beatles, but I seemed to be a magnet when it came to people who had encountered the Fab Four in one way or another. One of my bosses at Hemlock Printing had once worked as a bartender in London and told me he was always serving the Beatles drinks. Another guy I'd worked with had grown up in Liverpool and told me that as an eleven-year-old, he had saved his allowance for three months to purchase the new *A Hard Day's Night* album that was coming out. The night of his big purchase, he said his fifteen-year-old sister was babysitting him when her friends called to say the Beatles were at a party just down the block.

"I grabbed my album and raced down the street to the party," he told me, pausing to let the enormity of his good fortune sink in before continuing. "I got signatures from all four band members."

Peter's story was much more somber. He explained that he had grown up in New York City and as a teenager lived across the street from the Dakota building where John Lennon and Yoko Ono lived.

"I was in the living room watching an episode of *Quincy*

when I saw John and Yoko get out of a car," he recounted. "Then I heard a gunshot, saw John Lennon fall, and watched Yoko Ono kneel over him.

"I had to give a statement," he added. "I'm in the police report."

I was amazed by Peter's story. As an avid Beatles fan, I could recall the exact moment I learned of John Lennon's murder. I was fourteen and was getting ready for school when I heard the news on the radio. It was incredible to think that Peter had witnessed his assassination.

We spent the rest of the evening in easy conversation. For those few hours, I forgot about Jeremy, Dave, and my dysfunctional family. I even forgot about my roller-coaster year with the lottery win. I was just a guy enjoying the holidays with my newfound friends.

After years of Christmas nightmares, Bill had given me the gift of the best Christmas holiday I had ever experienced. And it was followed by another gift he delivered when he called to report that Jeremy's bank accounts in both Canada and the US had been frozen and his balance showed sixty-four cents.

Given all the damage Jeremy had done, I couldn't wait to drive in the nail.

I whipped out my phone and pounded out a taunting text.

"Hey, Jeremy, I hear your bank accounts were frozen with sixty-four cents. How about if I lend you another sixty-four cents? It will double your net worth."

18

It felt like I was stuck in the Twilight Zone. But in actuality, I was back in an Arizona courtroom, where Andre—Jeremy's former attorney—was now being grilled on the stand, accused of causing Jeremy's legal troubles through negligent representation.

The current nightmare had started in early February, when Jeremy's new attorneys filed a motion to dismiss the preliminary injunction and reconsider the contempt of court order, arguing that Andre hadn't told Jeremy of the November 25 temporary restraining order. They claimed that Jeremy didn't learn of it until I had sent over a copy to Jacob on December 10, three days after Jeremy had signed the paperwork that resulted in the $200,000 mortgage on my office building.

Just when I thought I had Jeremy cornered, he was once again slithering through the cracks, this time trying to beat the system by throwing his former attorney under the bus.

It was such an outrageous accusation, I was having a hard time staying hinged.

"That's bull#*@%!" I seethed when I heard the news. "There's no way he didn't know. How can that scumbag keep pulling this crap?"

Bill assured me that we would take him down in court. But in the back of my mind, I couldn't help but wonder if Jeremy could con Judge Whitten into buying his lies. I knew that if he did, we would be starting from scratch.

Bob Mills, Jeremy's newest attorney, launched into his courtroom attack on Andre by remarking on his friendship with Bill—making the ludicrous assertion that the two of them were working together to discredit Jeremy.

It was such a ridiculous, low-blow tactic that it probably hurt Jeremy's attorney more than it helped. But then he moved on to the one possible weakness in Andre's defense, the fact that he had never provided Jeremy with a written copy of the TRO. And when Andre pushed back, stressing that he had carefully reviewed the TRO with Jeremy during a November 25th phone call, Bob pulled out the clueless Canadian card.

"You knew Jeremy and Amy were Canadian citizens," Bob stated to Andre in an accusatory tone. "You had no reason to assume they had an understanding of US law."

I could see Andre stiffen and feel his disgust as he politely but firmly pushed back against Bob's assertions a second time, stating that he had walked Jeremy through the list of assets on the TRO and had carefully explained its implications during their half-hour phone discussion immediately following the hearing.

I watched Judge Whitten's face, trying to get a read on his reaction to the preposterous claims that Andre dropped the ball with his client and was acting in collusion with Bill to take down Jeremy. His face was expressionless but I hoped he was savvy enough to see the situation for what it was. From my viewpoint, it was obvious: Andre had endured repeated lies from

Jeremy in the month he served as his attorney. Now, because Andre had refused to compromise himself by continuing to represent such a low-life scum, Jeremy was doing everything he could to destroy his career.

Unfortunately for Andre, he was now discovering the reality I had been dealing with for months: Jeremy wasn't just a serial thief and pathological liar. He was a leech that permanently attached to his victims, sucking the life out of them long after the initial damage was done.

I had survived such an onslaught of shockwaves in the three months since the December 22 hearing that I was struggling to get a grip. I felt like I was walking across a booby-trapped desert. No matter how many landmines Bill and I managed to find and disarm, there were countless more ready to explode.

Though it now seemed like a distant past, January had kicked off on a high note. Thanks to the preliminary injunction Judge Whitten had issued, Jeremy no longer had access to any of my assets. He had been forced to turn over the two Porsches for safekeeping, and all company bank accounts were frozen, prohibiting him from further draining the company coffers or transferring money across the border. On top of that, he no longer had access to anything pertaining to KULT Labs. A receiver had been appointed to take charge and determine what assets could be preserved or liquidated for creditors. Between all of this and the $10,000 a day contempt fine Jeremy was being charged by the court, I figured it was only a matter of weeks—or even days—before everything was resolved.

But then came the motion to reconsider the contempt order and dismiss the preliminary injunction. And while Bill was preparing to knock down that roadblock, he began uncovering one fraudulent scheme after the next.

The deception was so pervasive it was hard to keep up with it all.

While sifting through Jeremy and Amy's bank statements, Bill's team discovered that prior to my cash infusion of $150,000 in late April 2015, the couple had less than $1,100 to their names. Yet within weeks of my initial investment, Jeremy was driving the white Mercedes convertible he would eventually gift to Shirley. Though Jeremy had told me that the company and patents were already in place prior to my involvement, no KULTiD patent existed. What's more, a search conducted by Snell and Wilmer early on found that KULT Labs hadn't been incorporated until June 25, 2015. This was more than a month after Jeremy presented me with the contract featuring a KULT Labs Incorporated logo, which offered me shares equivalent to a five percent stake in the company in exchange for my capital investment.

The bombshells just kept coming.

A late August 2015, letter written by Ross Richardson on Jeremy's behalf revealed that Jeremy was working in the US illegally. And while combing through payroll documents, Bill's team discovered that neither Jeremy nor Amy had paid a dime in income tax—either to the IRS or the Canadian government. If that weren't enough, his team discovered that between late April and mid-December, Jeremy and Amy had drained the company of approximately 1.5 million dollars, which they promptly transferred to a Canadian bank account and then spent.

My gut burned as I digested that news. I knew they had taken a lot. But more than a million dollars? I was so bitter I could taste bile as I thought about my efforts to have criminal charges filed against Jeremy and Amy following the launch party. "We've got bigger fish to fry," was the answer I had received. "You'll have to take it up in civil court."

I was being dragged through the sewer called Jeremy. And it was impossible to escape his stench. It didn't matter how big or wide his pile of crap got. He seemed to be free to crap wherever and on whomever he pleased. It was as though he had been given a golden pass by law enforcement. There was so much evidence of his crimes, he should have been rotting away behind bars. Instead, he and his parents were living in my houses, driving my cars and spending my money—while I waited for the civil justice system to do its job.

"No wonder he keeps getting away with it," I fumed to Mike as we counted the weeks to Jeremy's reconsideration hearing. "Criminals get treated better than victims."

I tried to distract myself and hold onto my sanity by making frequent trips home to visit Conway Kitty, throwing myself into my rare car obsession, and indulging in tropical vacations and sporting events. As a kid, I'd fantasized about attending professional ball games, especially the NFL. And now, with piles of money at my disposal, I was determined to turn those fantasies into reality. I flew to California to take in a Lakers game, and then headed to Dallas to see the Cowboys play. I knew how fortunate and blessed I was. But Jeremy was never far from my mind. I vacillated between depression and rage whenever I thought about that scumbag and his family blatantly stealing my money and thinking they could get away with it. And as the day of the hearing neared, another ingredient wormed its way into my emotional cocktail: panic.

I knew the evidence we had gathered against Jeremy was overwhelming. But I also knew how smooth and convincing Jeremy could be. He was like the devil himself, and if anyone could get Judge Whitten to bite the poisonous apple, it was him.

The one fear I couldn't shake was that Jeremy's knowledge of the TRO was coming down to a "he said, he said" confrontation.

But that all changed two and a half weeks before the reconsideration hearing. On March 10, Bill was notified of secret audio recordings Andre had made that captured Jeremy admitting to his knowledge of the TRO and its ramifications the day it was issued.

It was as though an angel had stepped in to ensure the truth prevailed. I was so blown away it took a minute or two for the enormity of the news to sink in. When it did, I erupted in a victory chant.

"We've got him!" I shouted to Mike, who had been by my side since the Jeremy nightmare started. "That lying scumbag is going down!"

❖

Mike and I patiently waited for Bob, Jeremy's attorney, to address the audio recording during his grilling of Andre, curious as to how he was going to try to wiggle his way out of it.

For the most part, Bob skirted around the contents, instead arguing that Andre had deceived his client and had tried to set him up through the secret recordings. He also suggested that Jeremy might have been confused by the conversation. But Andre wasn't taking the bait.

And when it was Bill's turn to cross-examine him, Andre made it clear that he had only made the recordings in an effort to protect himself.

"I felt Jeremy was becoming increasingly dishonest and felt that the day might come where I would be sitting in this chair," he explained.

His words landed with a punch and I could feel the satisfaction seeping through me as Andre stepped off the stand and headed to a bench in the courtroom to watch the rest of the proceedings. But that feeling evaporated the minute I heard Jeremy called to the witness stand.

I hadn't seen him since the November 1 launch party, and

though I had tried to mentally prepare for this moment, there was no way to suppress the rage that surged to an immediate boil the second I set eyes on him.

Jeremy was dressed in a high-priced, cream-colored designer jacket I knew my money had financed. It covered a bright shirt and came complete with a handkerchief in the pocket. He looked like he was headed to a Hollywood premiere.

My hands turned sweaty and balled into fists as I watched him make his way to the witness stand. He walked with a slight hunch, as though his back were hurt. I knew it was all part of his act to gain sympathy and it had me steaming with rage. My internal inferno intensified further when he took his seat and vowed to "tell the truth, the whole truth, and nothing but the truth."

I could also feel Mike heating up next to me as Jeremy began spewing his smooth-talking lies, portraying himself as an innocent, confused businessman from Canada who was working hard to build a viable business and just wanted to do right by his employees.

I had warned Mike that Jeremy was good at this, but I could see his disbelief as Jeremy launched into his act.

"He's like an actor vying for an Academy Award," Mike muttered under his breath. "It's like he was born to play this role."

I forced myself to shut out Jeremy's voice and lies—knowing that Bill would soon expose him for the piece of human waste he was. Instead, my thoughts locked on the last scumbags who had stolen from me and believed they could get away with it.

Coco, my beautiful blue-fronted Amazon parrot, had started out as the beloved pet of my friend Wendy, whom I'd met while selling supplies to the printing press shop where she worked.

Wendy had pictures of Coco plastered on her office wall and

I was immediately drawn to them.

"I've always wanted one of those birds," I told her as I admired the pictures. "I used to call them pirate parrots as a kid."

Coco became the center of our conversation each time I delivered supplies to the shop over the next eight months. I didn't think anything more of it until I received a phone call from Wendy out of the blue.

"This is a personal call," she said, her voice quiet and serious. "I've been battling cancer for the last ten years and it's back with a vengeance. It's now in my bones and I only have a few months left. I'm wondering if you would take Coco."

I was so stunned it was hard to know where to start. Wendy was a beautiful, divorced mother in her early forties at best. She was vibrant, funny, and kind. How could she be dying? And why would she choose me to take her beloved Coco?

"What about your daughters?" I managed after regaining my composure.

I could almost hear Wendy shaking her head.

"They can't," she responded. "They're in college."

My mind was racing. Though I had never actively sought out a parrot, I had often thought it would be fun to have one and there was no question that I was a full-fledged animal lover. It was devastating to think that Wendy was dying and being forced to part with a bird that had become her family. At the same time, I knew that it would make her feel better to know that Coco was in good hands.

"Well, I have always wanted a parrot," I said finally. "I'll tell you what. I'll come meet her and if she takes to me, we can go from there."

A few days later I was in Wendy's house, getting to know Coco. I immediately liked her. She was beautiful, with perfect markings, and, like Huey, she had spunk. I gave Wendy $750, insisting that I wanted to pay something, and then packed up Coco's cage and headed for the door. As I walked away, Coco called out the words that crushed my heart. "Bye, bye, bye."

I kept my eyes glued to my truck and continued walking, knowing that if I turned around, I would lose it.

It took time for Coco to warm up to me. A full month passed before she was comfortable enough to step onto my fingers. And it took several more weeks before she would go on my shoulder. But within six months, she was my bird.

Huey was slower to embrace Coco and I once caught them in a full-on Mexican standoff. But eventually, we all became a family.

Coco was smart and intuitive and she quickly became the life of the party. She mastered the sound of both cell phones and landlines and was so good with her imitation that she often sent people scrambling to answer their phones. I taught her the theme song to Gilligan's Island, which she proudly repeated when friends were around. But her biggest hit was the Stevie Wonder song "I Just Called to Say I Love You," which I continually played for her until she had memorized the words. She would turn her head side to side, like Stevie Wonder does, as she crooned the words, sending everyone rolling in laughter.

We were together nearly five years when I decided to change jobs. By this time, I was working at an equipment sales company in Calgary but had landed the position with Hertz and needed to move back to Edmonton—where I was living when I first acquired Coco.

The new job started immediately and because I needed time to find a house, I boarded Coco at an exotic bird shop in Edmonton and slept on Daryl's couch.

I had been a frequent customer of the shop prior to my move to Calgary and knew that Paul, the owner, would take good care of Coco while I was in transition.

What I didn't expect in a million years was the frantic early morning phone call I received from him Monday, May 29, the day I had planned to pick up Coco.

"Where have you been? I've been trying to reach you," Paul said in a tone that sent anxiety shooting through me. "Saturday night my place was broken into. They only stole one bird—it was your bird.

"I think I know who it is," he continued before I could fully digest his news. "There was this woman, about the age of forty, who was in here with her daughter who looked to be around twenty. They both had strong French-Canadian accents. They wanted to buy your bird. I said, 'Trust me on this, he will never sell.'

"They said okay, but they were very disappointed. I really think it was those two who stole Coco."

I was so livid I was shaking. What kind of people stole someone's pet? This wasn't just any bird. This was Coco and I wasn't going to let them get away with it.

I met the police at Paul's shop and immediately filed a stolen property report. But they made it clear that was the end of it—even after I pointed out that it was a theft of a pet valued at more than $3,000.

"I'm sorry, but we're not in the business of hunting down birds," one of the police officers explained. "We don't search for pets."

I headed home and launched my own massive hunt for Coco. My friends helped me post fliers around town that contained Coco's picture and a plea for help in finding her.

I also began scouring Craigslist and other for-sale posting sites, hoping that maybe they were just in it for some quick cash and had decided to sell Coco.

But nothing materialized.

I had a hole inside of me that grew bigger each day Coco

was gone. I had Huey for support, but my house felt silent without Coco's welcome or songs.

After six weeks of searching and heartache, I forced myself to accept the reality that Coco was gone and did my best to get on with my life.

Five months after Coco's disappearance, I was at the local Ford dealership getting the oil changed in my truck and had just walked out of the building when I heard the sound of a parrot. Then I heard it again.

My heart immediately began palpitating. I was like a mother hearing her lost child in a throng of kids. I knew that sound anywhere.

My eyes flew over the parking lot, trying to identify where the squawks were coming from. They were getting louder by the second and I realized they were coming from the direction of the Tim Horton's donut shop located behind the dealership.

I spotted three cars waiting in the drive-thru and as I started moving toward them, I realized that the squawks were coming from the second car, a blue mid-eighties Chrysler K.

A rush of adrenaline shot through me. I knew I had to get there before that car made it through the drive-thru. I had just one small problem: A few weeks earlier I had severely injured the sciatic nerve in my back, making it a painful struggle to walk.

I began hobbling my way across the parking lot, throwing out frantic prayers in my mind. *Please, God, let me get there in time. PLEASE.*

The pain was so intense I had to stop every seven or eight steps to recover. I kept my eyes locked on the first car in the drive-thru, desperately hoping that their order was a big one and would take a while to fulfill.

I pushed my body harder, willing myself to shut out the shooting pain as I inched my way closer. After what seemed like an eternity, I made it to the blue Chrysler, which, miraculously, was still trapped between the two others.

My sales persona instantly took over. I hobbled up to the car, knocked on the driver's side window and waved, forcing a friendly smile on my face.

A woman, clearly surprised, rolled down her window. She looked to be around forty, with a short black hairdo that framed her plump face. Next to her sat a thin woman wearing a pink hoodie who I guessed to be about twenty. And there, sitting on her shoulder, was Coco.

My heart was pounding so hard I could hear it. I jammed my fingernails into the palm of my hands to steady myself as I quickly assessed the situation and calculated my next move.

"I heard your bird and I'm just a huge bird nut," I said, continuing to smile widely. "What's your bird's name?"

The woman, clearly caught off guard by my sudden intrusion, uttered the word "Coco" in a strong French-Canadian accent.

That was it. In a split second, my arm was through her car window. "Come on, Coco," I coaxed. Coco immediately climbed onto my arm and I quickly pulled it out of the window.

"This is my parrot," I snapped to the stunned woman as Coco climbed onto my shoulder and nestled against my ear. "You stole it from Baker's Feed and Seed and I have the May 29 police report to prove it."

I took off before the woman could respond, limping my way back across the parking lot to the Ford dealership. I knew the woman would be coming for me as soon as she made it through the drive-thru and I wanted to be back in the safety of that building.

I knew the manager at the dealership and immediately sought out his help.

"Andy, this is the bird that was stolen from me five months ago. I know in situations like this, possession is nine-tenths of the law. Let's hide her."

Within minutes the two women from the drive-thru stormed into the dealership showroom, spitting out a string of curse words and demanding I give back the bird.

Now that I had Coco safely in my possession, I wasn't even fazed.

"I called the police and they are on their way," I announced calmly. "I can prove this is my bird."

The older woman exploded with another round of profanities.

"I'm going to get my husband down here and he's going to kick your ass," she screeched.

She looked like a half-crazed bat out of hell.

"Save your husband the trip," I replied. "You can kick my butt right now. I have a sciatic nerve injury so it won't be hard."

The mother and daughter stomped out of the dealership showroom and drove off. When the constable who had taken my stolen property report arrived a few minutes later and heard the story, all he could do was laugh. "Well, the good thing is that you've got your bird back," he said when he finally caught his breath. "I've been a police officer for fifteen years and that's the craziest story I've ever heard."

I got Coco home and spent the evening reconnecting with her.

But our reunion didn't last long. Three months to the day I got her back, I came home from work to find her dead.

I was so beside myself with grief that I howled like a baby. I had expected Coco to outlive me and the idea that she was gone after I had miraculously found her was too much to handle.

Paul later concluded that she must have been fed garbage food by the French Canadians, who I now viewed as pet killers.

Like Jeremy, they had stolen more than my property. They had taken a piece of me.

The pain from the memory was still so intense it felt like a knife was being twisted in my gut right there in the courtroom, where Bill was now beginning his cross-examination of Jeremy.

I could feel my revenge gene kicking into gear as Bill started volleying questions at him —quickly poking holes in his "I didn't know" defense. Bill's fit, five foot ten frame, dark hair, scholarly glasses and tightly trimmed beard made him look more like a college professor than a cut-throat attorney. He looked so disarming that people didn't see him coming. And I couldn't wait for him to tear into Jeremy.

Even without Andre's secret audio recording, there was plenty of direct evidence to suggest that Jeremy was well aware of the TRO and its ramifications when he sought out the $200,000 mortgage on the office building.

There was the fact that Jeremy had disclosed to Andre that he had sold the Ferrari and Audi R8 when they talked directly after the November 25 TRO hearing, indicating that Andre had reviewed the contents of the TRO with him.

There was an email from Andre to Jeremy dated December 4 that referenced a December 3 conversation reiterating that Jeremy needed to sequester the proceeds from the car sales—which further implied knowledge of the TRO and its implications. And this email arrived three days before Jeremy signed the mortgage documents for my office building.

There was a heated December 10 email exchange between Bill and Andre, in which Bill demanded to know if Jeremy was violating the TRO by taking out a mortgage on the Scottsdale house, with Andre responding that he had talked with his client and that Jeremy was doing no such thing. This, according to Jeremy's testimony, was the day he found out about the TRO from Jacob. Yet, Jeremy testified that he at no time asked Andre about it. Nor did Jeremy disclose that he had taken out the mortgage on the office building, even though—by his own admission—he was now fully aware of the TRO and what it entailed.

And if all of this evidence wasn't damning enough, there was also the fact that Jeremy didn't appear in court on either December 17 or December 22 to protest the contempt motion or to raise the claim that he was unaware of the TRO at the time he took out the $200,000 mortgage.

The secret December 16 audio recording, which Andre had made after Bill had notified him of the illegal mortgage on my office building, was simply the icing on the cake when it came to exposing Jeremy's lies.

Despite the mounting evidence against him, Jeremy stayed cool and composed as Bill asked him to read his response when Andre prodded him about their TRO conversation on November 25.

"Yeah, I remember that," Jeremy said, reading from the audio-recording transcript Bill had given him. "And I remember you saying to me that we would have to go back to the judge to get, you know, permission or…or whatever, in order to, you know, leverage, you know, the properties, and you know, get…get financing, and…and stuff like that."

Next, Bill directed Jeremy to another part of the December 16 transcript in which, after some prompting by Andre, he finally discloses that he took out the mortgage on the office building on December 7. In the transcript, Andre was clearly taken aback by Jeremy's disclosure.

"So this happened after…after we had conversations about… about the TRO and specifically about…about the houses and the building? This…this was in the works?" Bill said, reading Andre's words. Bill then locked his eyes on Jeremy.

"And what did you say in response?"

Jeremy didn't miss a beat as he read his words. "Yes, yes. It was in the works."

The courtroom was quiet after the exchange and for the first time in months, I could taste victory. We had so much evidence on our side it seemed a given that we would prevail.

And the best part was that Bill was just getting started. He was using the hearing as an opportunity to lay the foundation for our case against Jeremy—publicly exposing his insidious lies and cons that had enabled him to steal millions of dollars from me.

Through a series of pointed "yes" or "no" questions, Bill forced Jeremy to admit that he and Amy had taken upwards of 1.5 million dollars out of the company in an eight-month period and had failed to pay any income tax to either the US or Canadian governments. He also got Jeremy to admit to pulling $80,000 out of the company in early November—when company finances were precarious—to use as a down payment on the Oceanside condo.

Earlier in the hearing, Jeremy's attorney had argued that his client had used a big chunk of the mortgage proceeds to cover payroll and was too poor to repay the money. But Bill quickly dismantled this argument, illustrating Jeremy's continued lavish lifestyle in the three and a half months since the mortgage was taken.

He used social media photos and credit card statements to show that Jeremy was living it up in Southern California with his family at the same time Judge Whitten issued his contempt of court ruling. And if that wasn't enough of a slap in the face, Bill was able to prove that in both late December and early January, Jeremy had spent tens of thousands of dollars funding two all-expense-paid trips to Disneyland. The first was for Jeremy's complete extended family, which included Dave and Shirley; his sister Jenny and her husband, Ryan Davis; and their three kids. The second trip was for Amy's entire extended family, which included her parents, Pastor Dan MacGillivray and his wife, Bonnie; her brothers, Dan Jr. and Rob; their wives; and their combined seven children. Both vacations—which of course included Jeremy, Amy, and their two daughters—covered roundtrip airfare from Canada, hotels, Disneyland passes, and all food and incidentals. On top of all of this, Bill submitted evidence that Jeremy had spent more than $40,000 since late December and had recently enjoyed a ski vacation with Amy in Canada.

The vacations, all documented through photos that Jeremy and Amy posted on Facebook, represented such blatant, in-your-face spending that even Judge Whitten couldn't resist commenting.

"So, you mean he's poor like Kanye West poor," the judge snidely remarked.

Despite Bill's barrage of irrefutable evidence of his crimes, Jeremy maintained a straight face and continued his Academy Award-winning performance. But I knew he was squirming on the inside when Bill began prodding him about the properties.

Bill first got Jeremy to confirm that he had pledged the two houses and office building as collateral for my first $2.6 million investment, and had agreed in writing that my name would appear on the property titles. Then Bill drilled down on the July 2 email Jeremy sent me, in which he stated that my name couldn't be on the Arizona property titles because I hadn't been there at the time of signing.

"Who told you that?" Bill asked Jeremy pointedly.

"Our title company," Jeremy responded.

"Who at the title company told you that?" Bill persisted.

"I can't remember," Jeremy replied.

Every muscle in my body clenched as I listened to Jeremy's cretinous responses. But I loved it that Bill had him up against a wall and wasn't letting up.

"When were you told that?" Bill continued.

"I don't recall," Jeremy replied. "I never saw him; we talked on the phone."

"Actually, I was told by two different companies—a man and a woman," he added, clearly trying to cover his bases given that the property closings had been facilitated by two different companies.

Bill repeated Jeremy's outlandish claims for effect, and then continued with his line of questioning. He directed Jeremy to the next exhibit—an email he had received from an attorney at the Canadian law office in Edmonton where Shirley worked when she helped facilitate the purchase of the Sherwood Park home.

Bill read the attorney's email for the court.

"Hi Jeremy—we have received the registration. Somehow your partner's name was not included in the title. Here's a document so we can get all three of you on the title."

Then he looked at Jeremy.

"What was your response?"

Jeremy was void of emotion as he read back his words to the court, "Please leave the title the way that it is. Thank you."

I wasn't sure whether to laugh or scream as Jeremy's year of relentless deception played out for Judge Whitten. I was grateful that Bill had stripped Jeremy naked for the whole courtroom to see. At the same time, I was so humiliated and disgusted with myself for falling prey to Jeremy's repeated cons that it was hard to swallow.

The hearing, which had spanned two days, ended with closing arguments by each side on the morning of March 30. And by the end of the day, Judge Whitten had made his ruling.

In a scathing indictment, he detailed the irrefutable evidence pointing to Jeremy's lies, and lambasted him for his "inconsistent" and "inconceivable" claims of lack of knowledge during his testimony. Along with denying Jeremy's request to drop the contempt of court ruling, Judge Whitten refused to adjust the $10,000 a day fine, citing Jeremy's ongoing lavish spending and lifestyle as proof that he had money at his disposal. And a week later, on April 8, he denied the motion by Jeremy's attorney to dismiss the preliminary injunction.

It had been an emotionally grueling three and a half months and maddening as hell. But once again, we had Jeremy cornered.

19

Stories of Jeremy's cons and the trail of devastated victims left behind had been surfacing ever since the KULTiD launch party in early November.

But the volume and pace accelerated once the Canadian media got involved.

I was sitting in a Scottsdale hotel room in late March, mentally preparing for Jeremy's reconsideration hearing that would kick off the following day, when I received a phone call from Trevor out of the blue.

"Are you sitting down?" he asked as soon as he had me on the line.

I had been delivered so many blows by this point that I wasn't sure I could take another one—standing or sitting.

"No, I'm not," I replied, my gut automatically clenching. "What is it?"

Trevor laughed.

"It's gone national, dude! The story of your lawsuit against Jeremy has made the national news!"

The tornado of emotions that had been spinning and churning inside me for months had left me so drained and depleted I didn't know if I had anything left to feel. But Trevor's unexpected words were such a welcome gift they sent sparks of hope and excitement shooting through my body.

"Are you kidding me?" I managed as I reached for my iPad. "My case has made the news?"

I put Trevor on speakerphone while I typed in a Google search of my name. Within seconds, I had pulled up a national news report with the headline, "$50 M lottery winner Randall Rush sues Alberta company over investment." The news story was a straightforward account of my civil lawsuit against Jeremy, who had also incorporated KULT Labs in Canada. But as I read it, a new energy surged through me. After months of going it alone, my case was now on the radar of Canada's leading news organization. It was a huge shot in the arm and the emotional boost I needed because once some of the facts emerged, I knew it was only a matter of time before Jeremy was exposed as the lying, thieving scumbag he was.

"This is getting good," I raved to Trevor before hanging up the phone and whipping off an introductory email to the reporter. "Jeremy's going to have no place left to hide."

As much as it sickened me to think that I could be so thoroughly sucked in and taken by the Crawfords, I now knew that I was part of an unfortunate club that had dozens of members and branches that extended to Calgary, Edmonton, Kelowna, Toronto, Scottsdale, and Southern California.

In the five months since the KULTiD launch party, I had talked with numerous people who had been victimized by Jeremy and the Crawford family. It was like chasing a ball of unraveling yarn. Through my initial phone calls with people like Jim—the KULT Labs employee who had invested tens of thousands of dollars—I was provided with the names of others who had been screwed by Jeremy. They, in turn, provided me with more names of Jeremy's victims. I heard one story after the next of people who had been bilked out of their life savings, had their credit destroyed, or even lost their homes—all because they put their trust in Jeremy.

"He's got to be one of Canada's most prolific con artists," I vented to Mike after hanging up with yet another victim. "How does he keep getting away with it?"

I now knew that Jeremy had first cooked up the KULT brand in the spring of 2013 and had cheated numerous unsuspecting investors out of millions of dollars before he ever got his hooks into me. But from what I had pieced together, the KULT scam—which Jeremy had originally touted as a marketing, publishing, and production company before landing on the high-tech concept—was just the tip of the iceberg.

From what I could gather, Jeremy's scams dated back to the early 2000s, when he entered the magazine publishing business. I was told by people familiar with that con that Jeremy would convince unsuspecting business partners or employees to put up the operating capital, sell expensive advertising contracts based on a mock-up he slapped together, and then pocket the cash—oftentimes without delivering the promised magazine issue.

According to the information I received, he reinvented this con several times in both the Calgary and Toronto markets before moving to his next con: the construction industry.

I didn't know much about it. But I had heard rumors that he put up a website claiming deep expertise in both design and remodeling, and then he pocketed his customers' money sometimes without completing the work.

From there, it sounded like he moved into the multilevel marketing world, luring people into his downline by showing them fake high-dollar commission checks and making outlandish promises of instant wealth. Once hooked, his victims told me they were pressured into investing in one of his many scams or cosigning for a luxury vehicle his credit wouldn't qualify him for, sticking them with the ongoing payments.

I could taste the bile making its way up my throat when I thought about Jeremy and the lives he had so callously destroyed. But what had me burning most was his pattern of trolling churches for his prey. He had carefully groomed his deeply committed Christian facade: playing the piano for church congregations and repeatedly referring to God and his visions as a way to cast a wide net over his faith-driven victims. It made me sick to think of him prowling the Christian community and exploiting people's deeply personal spiritual beliefs to strip them of whatever he could.

I had uncovered most of these heartbreaking accounts through my ongoing outreach and sleuthing efforts. But people who had endured or were familiar with Jeremy's cons began seeking me out once the March 27 news story ran.

The first came through a Facebook message I received from a biker who told me his friend had been conned by Jeremy in a car scam a few years back. I had heard of so many cons Jeremy had pulled by this point that I couldn't even keep track of them all. But then he said something that caught my attention.

"He works with an older guy with one of those handlebar mustaches. It's the older guy who is calling the shots."

I had heard a similar statement from a Kelowna man who had been taken by Jeremy. This time, though, the comment was coming from a complete stranger—and the fact that he noted a handlebar mustache was unnerving.

I quickly messaged him a picture of Dave and asked him if he recognized the guy.

"That's him!" the man immediately replied. "That's the guy who works with Jeremy."

It didn't matter how much time had passed. The sting of Dave's betrayal was as painful and intense as that awkward encounter at the launch party when it hit me he was involved. I felt like the ex-military op in the movie *Source Code* who is forced to repeatedly go back in time, ride a bomb-ridden train, and endure being blown up over and over again.

Though I didn't know all the details, I had now heard enough stories and rumors to suspect that Jeremy—with Dave and Shirley as his complicit partners—had been sucking people dry both financially and emotionally his entire adult life.

It incensed me to no end.

Despite my headbanging frustration over the snail-paced speed of the court system, I was now convinced that it was only a matter of time before I was able to throw the Crawfords out of my houses in Scottsdale and Sherwood Park and reclaim at least some of my investment.

But I knew this was possible only because I had the money and time to devote to it. Though Jeremy's cons spanned every socioeconomic class and ensnared wealthy business owners and day laborers alike, the people I spoke with were either too financially or emotionally drained to take him on.

I was trapped in their same emotional hell and, had it not been for my deeply ingrained sense of right and wrong, I probably would have walked away from the fight as well. But now that I had come this far, I knew personal justice wouldn't be enough. I had to get redemption for everyone whose lives had been ripped apart by Jeremy. I also had to stop him from preying on anyone else.

I had been simmering over the challenge for months. Then the Canadian news story that had spotlighted my lawsuit against Jeremy planted an idea in my mind. If I could capture the victims' stories and detailed accounts of his serial frauds in a book and send it to every major news outlet and law enforcement agency in Canada and the US, Jeremy would have nowhere to hide. And even if he managed to stay out of prison, his name would be synonymous with Bernie Madoff, the reviled ex-Wall Street con artist who defrauded people out of close to a billion dollars.

I started asking around and discovered that Sandy, a friend of a friend, had a background in writing and research. I reached out to her and broached the idea of a book.

I started by giving her an overview of my case and Judge Whitten's scathing ruling against Jeremy. I also told her about the article that had been written and then began recounting some of the stories I had heard from other victims.

"I've already talked with dozens of people who have been scammed by Jeremy and there are more than enough stories for a book," I told her. "Jeremy is a serial con artist but he's like the Teflon Don. He keeps getting away with it and the only way to shut him down is to expose him to the world."

At first, Sandy hesitated. I sensed she saw it as more of a business deal gone south between Jeremy and myself and had no interest in getting involved. But I also felt she would change her mind when she realized that it was a much bigger story than just my own.

"At least talk with some of the people," I urged. "I want you to hear their stories."

After some nudging, Sandy agreed to make a few phone calls. As a starting point, I put her in touch with a group of victims in Calgary who had banded together after getting caught up in the multilevel marketing scheme run by both Jeremy and Amy.

The stories impacted Sandy enough that she decided to fly to Calgary for a few days and meet with the victims in person. By the time she returned, her attitude toward the book project had undergone a complete one-eighty.

Sandy told me that she had met with nearly a dozen

people over a two-and-a-half-day period, conducting in-depth interviews with each victim. She said they all had a heartbreaking story to share, and all brought along documentation to support their claims.

Their stories were strikingly similar. One after another, they recounted how they had been sucked in by Jeremy's charismatic personality, his carefully crafted appearance of wealth, his portrayal of a devout Christian family man, and his promises of riches if they entrusted him with their money. Some of them, who had borrowed money and leveraged their personal credit for Jeremy, were now in financial ruin. And all of them were emotionally devastated.

Though I had already heard some of these accounts and knew what they had gone through, I could still feel their pain cutting away like knives inside of me. There was one case in particular that affected me—it was that of an immigrant couple who could barely speak English.

They told Sandy they worked several jobs to save money for a down payment on a house and gave Jeremy the entire $6,000 they'd managed to scrape together.

"The fellow was so shy and sweet, and such a kind person," Sandy recounted. "Knowing that this couple was working incredibly long hours and rarely seeing their family, Jeremy told them that a little investment would bring them the financial relief they needed. This was 2012. They have never recovered."

There had been plenty of times in the past five months where I wanted to hunt Jeremy down and punch him in the face. But this was a new level of ruthlessness. How could any human being strip a struggling immigrant family of all they'd saved through years of eighty-hour work weeks and nonstop sacrifice? It was inconceivable.

After wrapping up her account of the Calgary trip, Sandy told me she would write the book. But before I could respond, she said there were some parameters she needed to make clear.

"This is only one side of the story," she stressed. "There will be another side. No one is all bad and this is going to be a balanced book."

A mix of calm and relief settled in as we discussed the details. Given everything I had experienced and heard to date, I suspected that what she would find was more of the same. But I, too, was adamant that it be an unbiased book. It had to be if I wanted to bring it to the attention of law enforcement. I just wanted the truth to come out, whatever the truth was. At this point, I felt it was my responsibility.

It was a sentiment echoed by my accountant, Max, who had become one of my closest confidantes.

"What are the odds of you winning the lottery? Like one in several billion?" he asked. "And what are the odds that Dave Crawford was one of your best friends and that his son would end up being one of Canada's biggest serial con artists?

"It's like you've come into this money because you are supposed to shut the Crawfords down."

Sandy and her colleague, Syd, began some initial digging and quickly discovered that one of Jeremy's key website claims—that he was the cofounder of *Alberta Oil*, an established, award-winning trade magazine—was completely false. They learned that Jeremy's only involvement was brainstorming the name and concept with a few other people he would eventually burn, pocketing the money from high-priced advertising contracts as he had done before, and then getting out by selling the concept well before any magazine was published.

On April 9, the same Canadian news organization that had published the initial article on my case picked up the story, running quotes from the current publishers that flatly disputed Jeremy's claim. That story also noted Judge Whitten's ruling in Jeremy's reconsideration hearing.

The floodgates were suddenly open. More victims of Jeremy's scams began reaching out to us and soon Sandy was inundated with new leads and information.

"I told you there was enough for a book here," I remarked to Sandy as I turned over the names of more people who had contacted me. "I think we've just opened Pandora's box."

20

I HAD BEEN SO CONSUMED BY my legal fight with Jeremy and the dark, festering emotions it triggered that I had forgotten I had anything to celebrate.

But my approaching fiftieth birthday flipped a switch inside of me. Given my DNA, my rough, dysfunctional childhood, and the trajectory I was on as a teen, it was a miracle I was still alive. But I had made it. And though I didn't have the wife and kids I had envisioned a fifty-year-old version of myself having, I had a gang of friends who had been with me through different aspects of my journey to the half-century mark.

I wasn't big on squandering money and given the $4.6 million gutting I had endured by the Crawfords, I was in a particularly cautious state when it came to protecting my remaining windfall. But I was ready for some fun with the people I cared about and I figured my fiftieth birthday was worthy of a splurge.

"It's okay to go a little sideways every once in a while," I reasoned with myself as I thought about other friends who had pulled out all the stops for their fiftieth. "This is one of those times."

For the first time in six months, I stopped obsessing about how to get even with Jeremy and Dave and began focusing on a fiftieth birthday bash that none of us would forget.

I knew it started with location. I didn't want the regular standbys of New York, Vegas, or Hawaii. That's what everyone else did. I wanted something unique—a place that people would be talking about for years to come. And that's how I settled on Iceland. It was far away and off the grid, and I had heard nothing but rave reviews about it.

"Dude, Iceland's been on my bucket list for years," one of my closest friends replied when I floated the idea. "Let's do it!"

My plan began to take shape. I invited twenty guys to join me for a five-day, expense-paid birthday bash near the end of June.

While Lisa worked to secure economy airfare and reasonably priced hotel rooms for everyone in the heart of Reykjavík, Iceland's capital, I concentrated on designing commemorative T-shirts for the event. The shirts, which listed every partygoer's name on the back, featured my head on Conan the Barbarian's body. It also featured the words "Seize the Day" and "I came, I saw, I conquered" inscribed in both English and Latin. The last quote duplicated the words my biological dad had tattooed on his arm—something I knew he would have appreciated.

I was already in full-on party mode by the time I boarded the plane that would take me to Toronto, our rendezvous point before continuing on to Iceland.

But as I settled in for the four-hour flight, the enormity of it all hit me. Jeremy or no Jeremy, I was entering my fifth decade as a multimillionaire. I was okay. I didn't have to worry anymore.

Even a year and a half after my lottery win, it was a struggle to grasp that this was now my reality. If only I could sit down with my mid-twenties self and assure him that it would all work out fine.

A boulder lodged in my gut as my thoughts traveled back to my twenty-sixth birthday, when I was so down on myself I wondered if life was worth living. That year, my mom had decided to surprise me by inviting over a few of my friends and hosting a small birthday party for me at her home.

I knew she meant well. But I was battling such a severe depression it was a struggle to get up in the mornings. The last thing I needed was an in-my-face reminder of just how much my life sucked.

My friends were getting married and establishing themselves in their careers. Yet despite everything I had done to get my life on track, I had nothing to show for it. I was jobless, had no relationship prospects, and was so broke I couldn't even afford a studio apartment. All I had was a beat-up '77 Dodge Dart and a couch to sleep on, thanks to the good graces of my friend, Barry.

"Good on you, man," I repeated as I moved from one friend to the next, forcing a smile as I congratulated them on their latest successes.

Inside, a piece of me was dying.

After that devastating night, I began viewing my birthdays as benchmarks of success or failure driven by two key factors: my finances and my romantic relationships. And for a while, I continued to strike out on both.

By the time my thirtieth birthday rolled around, my friends were buying houses and starting families. I was a grunt worker at a printing press shop—making $12.50 an hour after busting my butt for nearly four years.

"You're thirty and you've got nothing," the voice raged in my head as I pulled into the printing press' parking lot the evening of my birthday, ready to start my second shift of the day. I was so jaded I was nearly numb. My closest friends seemed to have everything they wanted drop out of the sky without giving it much effort or thought. I was on the other end of the spectrum, grabbing every overtime shift I could get and making sure I was the most productive worker in the shop. Yet, despite my workhorse mentality, both my professional life and my personal life were at a standstill.

I spent long nights staring at my bedroom ceiling in the small apartment I had finally managed to rent, reviewing my life and wondering when things would break my way. I had a fire burning inside of me and a do-or-die mentality when it came to success. I had to succeed. There was no alternative. I don't know where my intense drive came from—though I'm sure part of it was a reaction to growing up on welfare and having nothing. But I attributed a lot of my work ethic to my shop teacher, Mr. Reeves. He was an old-school get-her-done machinist who ran a trade program called Work Experience. It enabled my buddies and me to get real world experience through unpaid positions at local businesses, resulting in references that we hoped would help us land jobs after high school.

"If you do bad, I look bad—and if I look bad, I get mad," Mr. Reeves would drill into us on a daily basis. "If there is nothing to do, pick up a broom and sweep. Start cleaning crap."

It was a hard five years. But my eighty-hour work weeks and give-it-all-I've-got attitude finally began to pay off when I turned thirty-one. I decided to move from the Vancouver suburbs to Calgary—drawn both by a $2 per hour raise I was offered by another printing press company and the prospect of affordable housing. Thanks to the combination of the overtime money I had earned, the paid sick-leave days I had amassed, and the small retirement savings I had accrued, I had accumulated nearly $30,000 that I used as a down payment for a house. I still had no relationship prospects. But I was finally getting somewhere.

My next few birthdays marked a slow, steady climb out of my abyss. I moved from Calgary to Edmonton at the age of thirty-four, this time lured by a $5 per hour raise. And when I reached junior pressman status and maxed out my earning potential at $55,000 a year, I set my sights on a sales job at a printing supply company. I instinctively knew that sales was my destiny. I had a way of connecting with people and making them feel like they mattered. I noticed that the salespeople who showed up at our print facilities dressed nice, did a lot of talking, and spent a lot of time in their vehicles. It was like the position had been tailor-made for me. And the best part was that they earned upwards of $100,000 a year.

I chased the job hard for a year before I finally got my foot in the door. But once I got my hooks into sales, there was no stopping me.

As I continued my birthday time travel, the tension in my gut began to ease. True, it had been a rocky start, but I had proven to myself that I had what it took to succeed. I went from $75,000 as a print supply sales rep to a $100,000 a year job selling equipment rentals to the oil sector. Then I scored my golden ticket job with Hertz.

That's where I was working as I approached my forty-fifth birthday. I had never been big on birthday celebrations and didn't have any plans for this one. But as I moped around the office the week before, my supervisor noticed my birthday marked on the office calendar—a reminder that I was obligated to bring in donuts for the staff that day.

"It's a big one," he remarked. "What are you going to do?"

When I replied with my standard "nothing," my supervisor immediately pushed back.

"It's a big one," he repeated. "You should go to Vegas."

I didn't gamble so I didn't see the point. But out of curiosity, I did some research and noticed that Rush, one of my favorite bands, was playing there on my birthday. The first time I had seen Rush in concert was on my fifteenth birthday and it seemed to be a sign.

It was a spur-of-the-moment trip and I didn't have anyone to accompany me. But I had learned that if I wanted to experience a concert, a vacation, or anything else—I just needed to go for it.

The day of the concert I was enjoying lunch and a drink at a Wolfgang Puck in Vegas when the bartender began engaging me in conversation.

When I told him my name was Randy Rush and explained that I had come to Vegas to watch Rush for my birthday, he didn't believe me. For proof, I pulled out my driver's license.

"No way," the bartender exclaimed after looking it over. "That's crazy."

A group of long-haired guys wearing Rush T-shirts were seated at the end of the bar and overheard our exchange. They immediately sent over a couple of birthday drinks. As soon as I finished them, a few more drinks arrived.

Though I was sitting alone downing my drinks, I didn't feel alone. I felt like I was at a party being thrown on my behalf.

I finished my drinks and headed to the end of the bar to thank the guys and shake their hands. That's when they gave me the best birthday gift I had ever received.

One of the guys hoisted himself to a standing position on his chair and let out a loud whistle—getting the attention of every patron in the crowded restaurant.

"This is Randy Rush," he shouted as he motioned toward me. "He's here to see the Rush show and it's his birthday."

Everyone in the room let out a cheer. Then, as I waved

and moved toward the door, they erupted into chants. "Randy, Ran-dy, Ran-dy," they all yelled in unison. For those few minutes, I felt like a rock star.

I couldn't help but smile as I relived the memory. Back then I had worn a short, corporate haircut—a necessity for my job. But I had envied the long-haired guys with their Rush T-shirts. I had worn my hair long through high school and had vowed to grow it out again as soon as I retired. It was a vow I had made good on the minute I discovered my lottery win at the corner grocer in Lamont a year and a half earlier. I hadn't cut my hair since and hadn't even shaved. I looked like a cross between a rocker, a biker, and Grizzly Adams. I was finally my authentic self. And it felt amazing.

My forty-fifth birthday had been intense. But this one was going to be over-the-top. Twenty guys with five days of free time were descending on Iceland. It was going to be an explosion.

I thought I was bringing the party. But I was set straight the minute we exited our plane. The airport was a sea of soccer scarves and jerseys. There was so much excited energy in the air I could hear the electric buzz. Iceland's soccer team had just made it into the quarter-finals of the Euro Cup, a first in the nation's history. And the country was in pandemonium. It was a complete fluke that my birthday bash coincided with the event and we were ecstatic at our good fortune.

"Dude, it's like they knew it was your birthday," one of the guys hooted as we pushed our way to the taxi stand. "Unbelievable."

The city was in full-on party mode. After checking into our hotels, we headed to the city square to join throngs of half-crazed soccer fans in their chants and celebrations.

I had heard about Iceland's indescribable beauty and otherworldly landscape. But I couldn't have imagined the stunning scenery. It was a mix of volcanic rocks and steaming craters, endless aqua-blue natural pools, and breathtaking waterfalls all bordered by majestic snowcapped mountains. It was like landing on another planet—starting with the midnight sun. We arrived at the height of summer solstice, when the sun only set for three hours and nothing ever went dark.

The second day there, I booked a small bus for a private day tour through the countryside. We stopped by the Blue Lagoon, known for its healing properties, and took in the open craters and rolling lush green hills dotted with sheep. But my favorite was the waterfalls. They cascaded from one to the next and were so beautiful and mind-blowing they didn't seem real. Even for a bunch of smart-aleck party guys, we were at a loss for words. "Dude, unbelievable," was all we managed as we drove from one surreal setting to the next. "Holy cow."

My five-day Iceland party was filled with nonstop celebration, conversation, food, and fun. We were spread across several hotels but would meet up around lunchtime to kick off the day's activities. I donned my kilt and birthday T-shirt and roamed the city streets with my friends, using my fox-head purse as a makeshift puppet head to kick off conversations with any interesting people I met.

A private birthday dinner at a banquet hall I had rented for the occasion topped off the week. But as the end of our stay approached, I realized I wasn't ready to go home.

"Who wants to go to Ireland?" I asked as we wrapped up dinner the last night there. "It's on me."

Most of the guys had to return to their families and jobs. But five of us made the impromptu trip to Dublin for another week of celebration and sightseeing.

Ireland was personal for me because it was the home of my Rush ancestors. Other Irish descendants I knew who had made the trek told me it was like coming home. That's what it was like for me when I made a day trip to Cork. It felt so familiar and comfortable, I didn't want to leave.

The week in Ireland ended and I still wasn't ready to return to Canada. Instead, I suggested that we all head back to Iceland for a few more days to regroup and welcome home the soccer team. We had watched them play and lose in the semifinals while in Dublin. But having shared in the celebration and euphoria, it seemed only fitting to see it all the way through.

A day later we were back in Reykjavík's city square, where a stage had been erected to honor the returning players. At least 200,000 fans—more than half of the country's entire population—crammed the square and surrounding streets to show their love and adoration. It didn't matter that they had lost in the semifinals. They were national heroes.

It was a historic moment in Iceland's history, and I—the welfare kid from New Westminster who had once spent weeks collecting soda cans and Coke bottles to scrape together the money for that coveted Road Runner lunch box—had been there to witness it.

"Not bad for a fiftieth birthday bash," I noted as we settled into the plane for our flight home. "I'd say we did pretty well."

❖

My reprieve from Jeremy ended as soon as the plane touched down in Vancouver in mid-July. But after everything that had transpired since Judge Whitten's refusal to dismiss either the contempt of court ruling or the preliminary injunction, I knew the end was near.

The latest round in my chess match with Jeremy had started in late April, when Bill suggested we make Jeremy a settlement offer that would allow him to walk away from the hefty $10,000 a day contempt fine that had now amassed to more than $700,000. I wasn't interested in giving Jeremy any sort of break. But I knew we had to do something to end the stalemate, and as long as I stripped him clean of everything possible, I was fine with it.

"I want it all," I stressed as Bill put together the offer. "My assets, any remaining money, the company IP, the software app—everything."

Given the noose that was tightening around Jeremy's neck, I halfway expected him to cave. Instead, his attorneys declined my proposal and put two counter-settlement offers on the table.

After all the bulls#@! I had already been through with Jeremy, I should have expected more of the same. But just the idea that Jeremy and Amy thought they had bargaining power was so infuriating I wanted to punch in a few walls.

And that was before Bill started reading me their counteroffers. What they proposed was so ludicrous I wondered if Jeremy had turned to smoking crack.

Counter Option A had me paying Jeremy and Amy $10 million (in US dollars) for their remaining shares in KULT and all company ownership/IP. It stated that I would receive what was left of my office building and any available interest in the Oceanside Property, but that they would keep both houses and the cars.

In Counter Option B, they had me turning over all my shares and interest in the KULT companies to them. In return, it said Jeremy and Amy would sign over their interests in the Sherwood Park Property, the Scottsdale Property, the KULT Building, and the Oceanside Property. It specified that they would keep the business, the IP, and the vehicles, and that they would be given a ninety-day window to secure financing to purchase the Scottsdale house and KULT Building from me for the original purchase price.

Both options came with the added stipulation that I drop

my lawsuit against Ross Richardson, which Bill had put on the backburner while going after Jeremy.

I was a dragon breathing fire.

"I'm done!" I spewed after hearing the counteroffers. "They can go pound sand!"

Though Bill knew we had Jeremy against the wall, he also recognized that it could be a long-drawn-out proceeding and warned me that if we didn't try to negotiate a settlement agreement, the ongoing legal costs could get expensive.

But after the bloodsucking I had endured from Jeremy over the past year, I was ready to extract my own pound of flesh.

"I don't care about legal fees," I ranted. "It doesn't matter what it costs or how long it takes. It's the principle of it. I'm not quitting until I get everything."

The dialogue with Jeremy's attorneys went dark after that. We waited through the entire month of May without any action on Jeremy's part. By early June, the mounting judgment against him had topped $1.1 million and we knew we had Jeremy in a stranglehold. But we worried it was so crippling that Jeremy would never be able to pay it and we would be stuck in a never-ending legal nightmare.

To get things moving, Bill approached Judge Whitten with a purge offer for Jeremy if he would return the original $200,000 to the court. The proposal stipulated that Jeremy would still be responsible for the $450,000 fine that had amassed prior to February 4, when Jeremy's attorneys filed the motion for reconsideration of the contempt order. However, it wiped away the fine that had been accruing since March 30, when Judge Whitten upheld his initial contempt ruling. The flipside was that if Jeremy didn't comply, he would face the original judgment, which was now nearing $1.4 million, and a warrant would be issued for his arrest.

Just hearing the words "Jeremy" and "arrest" used in the

same sentence sent an energy charge surging through me.

"Can you just imagine that scumbag behind bars?" I said to my friends, reveling in the thought of him dressed in orange prison garb and locked in a small cell with only a cot and a toilet. "He'll be turning on those crocodile tears for real."

Judge Whitten agreed to Bill's proposal and signed the new order on June 13, giving Jeremy until the end of the day June 21 to turn over the original $200,000 that had landed him in contempt. To my joy, the national news media in Canada picked up the story. The article, titled "Jail threat looms for Edmonton man being sued by $50 M lotto winner," provided a recap of my ongoing legal battle with Jeremy and his continued shenanigans, noting that an arrest warrant would be issued if Jeremy didn't adhere to the orders.

"This is great," I gloated to Mike as I read the article, which included links to the previous stories that had been published. "I'll bet Jeremy is crapping his pants."

When Jeremy once again failed to comply with the court orders, it was clear Judge Whitten was through playing games. His attorneys had responded by filing for a stay while it went through the appeal process, but, at this point, we all knew it was over for Jeremy.

The next step in the legal process was for Bill to request a cause for civil arrest hearing, which Judge Whitten scheduled for July 18 and mandated that Jeremy be in attendance.

This was the hearing I was waiting for when I arrived back from my three-week fiftieth birthday bash. According to Bill, Judge Whitten had been visibly pissed off at the June hearing and was clearly done with Jeremy's antics.

But neither of us realized just how done Judge Whitten was until Bill showed up at the July 18 hearing and saw a sheriff's deputy waiting in the galley.

Despite Judge Whitten's mandate that Jeremy be present, he

was nowhere to be found. And that set the judge off.

"Where is Mr. Crawford?" Bill told me Judge Whitten had demanded, glaring down at Sean Woods, one of Jeremy's attorneys.

"He's in Canada, Your Honor," the attorney had responded. "But I could get him on the phone if you would like to speak with him."

Judge Whitten's response—as Bill recounted it to me—was such a long time coming it killed me that I wasn't there to hear it in person.

"Well, I can't very well arrest him over the phone, can I?"

❖

Bill was back in his neighborhood Safeway the following evening, grabbing a few items for dinner, when the call came from Jeremy's attorney.

"Jeremy is waving the white flag," Sean Woods said simply. "He's ready to give it up."

Bill, who had been expecting the call, was prepared with our list of demands.

"We are talking everything, right?" he stressed. "We are talking the houses, the office building, the vehicles, the KULT IP, Jeremy and Amy's shares—anything else that's left."

Jeremy's attorney, according to Bill, didn't miss a beat.

"Yes," he replied. "You get everything. It's done."

A mix of emotions churned through me as I listened to Bill deliver the victory news. I was relieved it was over and knew I should feel happy, or at least satisfied, that I was getting everything back that was left to get. But I was so bitter and angry that I was almost numb.

Bill set to work structuring the terms for the settlement agreement and establishing dates for me to reclaim my assets.

Knowing their freeloading days were over, Dave and Shirley vacated my Sherwood Park house by the end of July, and preparations were made for Jeremy and Amy to get out of my Scottsdale house and turn over the title to my office building.

Ross Richardson was next on my legal hit list, followed by Dave and Shirley—whom I planned to sue for back rent. I was also still determined to get justice for all of the other people who had been hurt by Jeremy and his family. But my legal battle with the scumbag was over. After nine months of slowly knocking out his bishops, his knights, and his pawns, I had finally cornered his king.

And that, at least, felt good.

"Checkmate, Jeremy," I could hear the voice in my head sneer. "Checkmate."

21

I HAD TO TAKE CHARGE OF my life. And I knew it started with taking charge of myself.

The reality hit me every time I looked in the mirror and saw a stocky, middle-aged rocker with an out-of-control beard and protruding gut staring back at me.

Three weeks of celebrating in Iceland and Ireland hadn't helped my physique any. But that was only the tail end of a year-and-a-half-long rocket ride fueled by on-the-go eating and drinking in whatever location I happened to land.

My insane travel binge and constant eating out—coupled with my strong Wells genetics—was a nasty combo that had packed an extra thirty-five pounds on my five-foot-nine frame.

I could hear my mom's needling, forty-year-old jab come at me each time I passed a mirror.

It was my tenth birthday and the family friends we were visiting had just presented me with a Mr. Big candy bar. This wasn't just any candy bar. It was a double-sized mound of vanilla wafers smothered in caramel, peanuts, rice crisps, and chocolate, and my mouth watered just thinking about it. I knew that if I waited until we left, Mom would exact her "mom tax," which often amounted to half of any treat I managed to secure.

I usually resigned myself to it. But this was my birthday gift and I was determined to enjoy every last morsel.

"Can I eat it now since it's my birthday?" I asked my mom in front of her friends, conjuring the sweetest voice I could muster.

We both knew I had cornered her into saying "yes," and I could feel the burn from the scalding look she shot me. When she spoke, her tone was cutting and sarcastic.

"Well, you enjoy that now, Randy," she said, drawing out her words for effect, "because when you hit adulthood, you'll look just like your dad."

I was such a scrawny, skinny kid I couldn't imagine ever being fat, but I knew that's what she meant by her derogatory remark. She had told me more than once that the Wells side of the family were all short and stout. My dad, who my mom said was fit and trim in high school, was already on the chunky side by the time he pulled up in his car to give us a ride when I was four years old. And true to her vindictive prediction, the weight kicked in for me when I hit my early twenties.

It had been a struggle ever since, though I always managed to reel it back in whenever I reached the brink and was teetering on the edge of no return. And I was definitely there now.

I spent a couple of days at my beach condo, contemplating my life and future. Between the money high, the Crawford low, and nonstop adrenalin rush of the past twenty months, I had let go of the controls and was shooting around like a ball in a pinball machine. And it wasn't working.

"Dude, you have got to get a handle on this," I could hear myself prod. "If you keep living like this, you are going to age real fast."

The same drive and discipline that had pulled me out of my hole two decades earlier stepped in and took over.

I needed a clean start, which I symbolized by grabbing a pair of scissors and a couple of heavy-duty razors and erasing my beard. Then it was on to my diet and lifestyle.

I enjoyed an occasional beer, but I knew it packed calories and was ready to give that up. I also knew I had to stop smoking. I had struggled with cigarettes since I was a teenager and had an ongoing love/hate affair with them.

I had gone cold turkey in my late twenties and had managed to stay off of them for seven years. I thought I had beat the addiction until a coworker who had recently returned from Cuba presented me with a cigar.

"Thanks, but I don't smoke anymore," I replied.

My coworker, a native from Poland, laughed.

"One cigar won't kill you, Randy," he quipped in his thick Polish accent.

We headed to the parking lot to light up. The second that nicotine hit my system, I was soaring.

"Oh, yeah, baby," I said, launching into my best impersonation of Krusty the Clown, the alcoholic from *The Simpsons*. I made my hand tremble like the cartoon character and let out a laugh. But inside, I knew there was a lot of truth to my act. I had been engaged in an ongoing battle ever since—with a year or two off, a few months on. I had been off them for a while when I hit Iceland but had used turning fifty as a reason to have just one.

I had been smoking ever since, and I knew it was time to stop.

I tossed my remaining cigarettes in the garbage and devoted myself to a strict ketogenic diet that removed all sugars from my menu and focused on lean proteins and low-starch vegetables.

It took a couple of weeks to break my sugar and nicotine cravings and get into the routine. But once I got myself on track with my clean diet and overall body cleanse, I shifted to the next to-do on my cleanup list: my finances.

Just thinking about the money mistakes I had made over the last year and a half was enough to trigger stabbing pains in my gut. And it wasn't only the Crawfords. I had also allowed myself to be cleaned out of another chunk of money—once again by a close friend.

Eight months earlier, I was having a few beers and laughs with Gary, who had flown down from Edmonton for the weekend, when he approached me with a business idea. He told me that he and a couple of other guys I knew from my time at Hertz had been working on a side project involving septic tanks.

"Sounds like a crappy business to be in," I joked.

Gary laughed with me but pushed on. "It's a system that uses reverse osmosis to treat the water and makes it so clean it can be put back into streams," he explained. "The demand for this is huge and the profit margins are close to fifty percent."

Gary told me that Ryan, who had worked as a manager at Hertz while I was there, had connections with a start-up company on the East Coast that had secured a patent on the reverse osmosis process and had granted them the rights to sell the system in Western Canada.

"We've already done nearly a dozen installations," he added, wrapping up his pitch. "We just need some seed money and operating capital to really send this soaring."

Despite having KULTiD blow up in my face, I was still craving a ground-floor opportunity in an innovative tech company. And Gary's words ignited that familiar energy charge inside me.

If this septic system could really turn sewer waste into

drinking water, I knew municipalities would be clamoring for it. And if the profit margins were what he said they were, it sounded like a slam dunk. And the best part was that I already knew and trusted the players.

Gary and I had met at Hertz several years earlier and had immediately bonded over our love of cars. We had developed a close friendship and often hung out together outside of work. We had even figured out that on the night my lottery numbers actually hit—two weeks before I discovered I held the winning ticket—I had crashed on his couch after a night on the town. Like me, Gary was a driven go-getter and was one of the top sales reps at Hertz. I knew that if anyone could close deals, it was him. Though I wasn't as close to Ryan and Brad, the third member of the business trio, I had interacted with them both at Hertz and considered them awesome guys with good heads on their shoulders.

"Okay," I said, "why don't you put together a business plan and I'll run it by my guys?"

Trevor, Mike, and Max, who had all helped me sort through the KULT nightmare and had reviewed other potential business opportunities on my behalf, did a thorough analysis of the business plan and gave me an enthusiastic thumbs-up.

Like me, Trevor knew and trusted the men involved, and he, Mike, and Max were all impressed by the strength of the business proposition. It had it all: the profit margins, the environmental benefits, and a built-in customer base that spanned all of Western Canada.

"I think this is as good as gold, Randy," Max said after crunching the numbers. "I would go for it."

I worked with Gary to structure a deal in which I invested money to cover equipment purchases and initial operating costs in exchange for a twenty-five percent stake in the company. I also reserved the right to take over management if I determined the company needed guidance. I had learned hard lessons from the KULT disaster and planned to stay actively involved in this business venture—though I couldn't imagine any issues. This was Gary we were talking about, and I was convinced he was going to knock it out of the park.

I had so much faith and trust in him that I gave him free rein. I just asked that he keep me updated on projects and incoming revenue and told him that Max, Trevor, and Mike were available to help if they needed assistance with accounting or operations.

"We'll check in every quarter to see where things are at and make adjustments if needed," I said. "Just do your thing and let's get this business booming."

Everything seemed to be going according to plan. Gary checked in with Trevor regularly to provide updates, and by the end of May he reported forty-two jobs on the books. It was like someone had turned on the flashlight in the dark tunnel I had been trapped in with Jeremy and delivered a much-needed emotional boost. But when I asked Gary for the quarterly financials so I could get a better sense of the revenue flow, he put me off.

"We're so slammed we've gotten a little behind," he explained. "Just give me a couple more weeks to pull it together for you."

I wasn't fazed at first. I trusted Gary completely and understood how such an onslaught of business could put them behind. But by the time my fiftieth birthday bash rolled around, my internal guards were beginning to kick in. Gary still hadn't turned over the books and when we landed in Iceland, he was evasive and distant—and midway through the five-day celebration, he disappeared for two days.

Trevor, who knew Gary as well as I did, was also becoming concerned.

"I don't know what's up with Gary, but something is off," he confided. "I have a bad feeling."

I was so caught up in my birthday celebration with the other guys I pushed it to the back of my mind. But by the time I landed back in Canada, the alarm bells had sounded. Despite repeated requests by Trevor, Gary still hadn't turned over the books. It was a déjà vu and I wasn't going to wait around. My gut was in knots as I dialed Trevor's number.

"You need to get in there now and find out what's going on," I fumed. "I need answers and if you don't do it, I'm coming up myself."

My gut was telling me it wasn't good. But I wasn't prepared for the news Trevor delivered.

"It's bad, Randy. They aren't doing crap; the books are a disaster and the money is pretty much gone."

His words hit me so fast and hard it was like my stepdad's open-hand palm strike all over again. Gary's glowing reports of booming business slammed from one side of my brain to the other.

"What about the forty-two jobs?" I managed, fighting back the rage making its way up my throat.

"All I can see are five," he replied.

Trevor told me that when he cornered Gary and demanded answers, the finger-pointing and blame-shifting began. Gary claimed that there was so much infighting between Ryan and Brad that he had spent most of his time playing interference. He couldn't explain away his gross exaggeration of the number of jobs booked or his false claims that business was booming when only five jobs had been completed over a six-month period. Nor could he explain the mismanagement of my investment. Despite the low volume of business, they had each been taking a $12,000 monthly salary and Trevor said the books showed other unaccounted-for withdrawals. My money was gone and there was nothing to show for it.

"This is like Jeremy all over again," I thundered into the phone. "Get in there and fire them now!"

At first, I hoped we could salvage the business. But when we started digging further, the full scope of the disaster materialized. Max discovered that the business owed nearly $20,000 in back taxes, and when we started examining the jobs that had been done, we found that none of them were to code. And a job that had been done for the County Strathcona was so shoddy they threatened to sue us. I was so sickened by it all it was hard to breathe.

"Just find someone who knows what they are doing, fix everything, make it right, and let's shut this down," I barked.

I hadn't talked with Gary since Iceland and was too destroyed by his lies and betrayal to ever communicate with him again. Like the Crawfords, I had let my love for Gary guide me. And though I thought I had this one buttoned down, I had once again been flushed down the toilet.

The worst part was that I had been warned about this nearly a year earlier by Derek, a former classmate who had since built a billion-dollar company and had offered to meet with me to discuss my finances.

"I know you don't want to hear this," he had said, "but friends, family, and business don't mix."

Though I had already sunk more than $4 million into KULTiD at that point and was beginning to suspect problems, I was convinced that if I extended a hand up to my friends, it would turn into a win-win. On top of that, Gary had such an incredible track record at Hertz that he seemed like a sure bet.

Rage and regret collided inside of me as I replayed the last year in my mind.

If only I had listened to Derek.

I had known the minute we sat down that I needed him on my team. He was a proven financial genius and I knew that if I could convince him to manage my money, I would be in great shape.

The bulk of my money was still sitting in the bank earning three percent interest. Steve, the bank VP, told me he managed the money for two other lottery winners—including a $37 million winner—and was generating safe returns for them every year. I realized a guaranteed three percent on tens of millions was a lot of money. But I also knew I could do better.

"I don't want to be risky but I've got to see numbers around the six to eight percent range," I had told him. "I've got to shop this around."

I had pitched Derek on the idea of managing my money during that initial conversation but he was still tied up in the day-to-day operations of his company. Now, though, he was mostly retired and agreed to work with me on a limited basis. He said it started with getting a snapshot of my current finances and investments to date.

"There are no wrong answers," he stressed. "But I need to know exactly what you've done with the money."

Talking about my investment screwups was so painful it was like swinging a sledgehammer on myself. But as I opened up to Derek and put everything on the table, a release valve opened inside of me. All the pressure that had been building was suddenly gone. Though I had done well with the cars and real estate I had purchased, I had been in over my head with the rest and I knew I no longer had to worry. Derek understood how to grow money. He had done it to the tune of a billion dollars and now had my back. It was like a gift from heaven.

Derek listened intently as I detailed my expenditures and investments to date and told him about my desire to grow my money, then set up a trust to help needy children and other vulnerable populations. I also told him about my goal to help returning missionaries get on their feet and to contribute to other causes that might interest me.

When I finished, I could see a smile breaking open across his face.

"Okay, that's not bad," he said, referring to the million-dollar max budget I had established for each of the four houses I had purchased. "I thought you were going to tell me you had dumped $5 million apiece into mega mansions."

Though Derek cautioned that giving financial gifts to friends and loved ones could backfire because some people don't value money they didn't earn, he admitted that he was touched by all I had done to help my friends—including putting them up in my houses for free. He said he was also inspired by my reasons for wanting to leverage the money I had won to the fullest extent possible.

"I like your nature and I like where your head is at," he noted. "I think I can work with you and help you accomplish what you want to do." For the first time since my lottery win, I was at peace. I was still in cleanup mode with Jeremy and knew that at least half of my investment in KULT Labs would never be recouped. I also knew I had to write off my loss with Gary and his crew. But I had survived the meteor crash mostly intact and I knew I was now on the right track.

With my high-level money management issues now solved, I only had one final issue to address: I needed a regular paycheck.

I hadn't realized how much I enjoyed receiving a paycheck each month until it went away. I missed the satisfaction of getting that monthly deposit in my checking account and knowing that it was my money to budget and do with as I pleased. I needed the structure and the discipline of working within a set budget.

When I explained this to Derek, he readily agreed.

"So how much do you need to live on?" he asked. "A million dollars a year?"

I hadn't really thought about it in terms of an annual salary and his question reverberated through my mind. How much was enough? How much did I really need?

When I was at Hertz, I had lived very comfortably on $200,000 a year. My life had accelerated in the twenty months since my lottery win—and now my old salary didn't seem like nearly as much. I had attorneys, accountants, and my assistant Lisa to pay, as well as friends I was helping and pet projects I wanted to pursue. I also wanted to continue traveling. At the same time, I owned my condo and log-cabin house outright—as well as all of the cars I had purchased. And a million dollars sounded excessive.

"I can live on a lot less than that," I replied finally, throwing out a number that worked for me. "I want to live comfortably—not extravagantly."

22

I HADN'T PLANNED TO GO TO Africa. But I couldn't shake the advice from a friend who had traveled there with her church.

"You need a reset, Randy," she had stressed. "Go to Africa, check out the schools, and meet the children and staff. It will give you the reboot you need."

Her words hit me at the core because I knew she was right. I had to do something to shed the bitterness and get back to being me.

It had been six months since I had cornered Jeremy into turning over all assets that remained from the KULTiD nightmare. But I was still stewing in anger and resentment. I knew I was lucky and should be filled with joy and gratitude over the enormous financial gift I had been given. But so far, my $50 million windfall had brought as much grief as it had joy. More than anything, it had shown me the ugly side of greed, which had eroded several friendships and my overall trust in people.

"You've got to get a handle," I repeated to myself every time

I felt the rage creeping in. "This isn't the way to live life."

I had done my best to strip off my war armor and get back to my fun-loving self. I had even gone as far as flying to Arizona with my friend Kurt for a Halloween bash in which we donned Batman and Robin costumes and cruised around Phoenix in my very own Batmobile, an exact replica of the superhero's crime-fighting car that I had purchased from a rare car dealer a year and a half earlier.

It was the kind of extravagant fun that a pile of money bought. But the emotional high was short-lived.

Two weeks later I received news that my stepdad was suffering from cancer, and as I flew him to a specialty clinic in Mexico to access the experimental treatment he needed, I found myself contemplating my purpose in life.

What if I got cancer? What if I died suddenly? What would I want my legacy to be?

I had been working with Derek on my long-term plan to set up a trust in which all generated interest would be used to help suffering children around the world and support other causes I cared about. But I wanted something I could sink my teeth into now—something that had a long-term positive impact. And when friends from my new church told me about the schools they operated in East Africa to help some of the most vulnerable children there, it immediately piqued my interest.

"So how much do you need?" I asked one of the project leaders when she told me about a parcel of land they hoped to acquire in Uganda for the new high school they wanted to build.

I knew from our conversations that the high school initiative was coming on the heels of a newly constructed primary school—which made the new round of fundraising more challenging. Even before asking the question, I sensed that I would be footing the bill.

Now that Derek was managing my money, I no longer had access to unlimited cash. But what I did have was a fleet of rare cars I had purchased since my lottery win.

And I realized in that moment that one of them—a Ferrari 430 Scuderia that had been designed in collaboration with Formula One race car driver Michael Schumacher—was going to fund that project.

A sense of peace and happiness washed over me as I thought about the relief and joy my gesture would bring.

"Consider it done," I replied after she told me how much the land would cost. "Just give me a couple of weeks to auction off one of my cars and I'll get you the money."

❖

The words "you need a reset" reverberated through my mind as I boarded a plane for Uganda in early February 2017, virtually two years to the date of my lottery win. It wasn't just my friend nudging me to go. I had also been encouraged to make the trip by the people who oversaw the Christian-based school projects there.

"Giving money is one thing, but you need to experience it in person," they urged. "Visit our new primary school and other education projects and meet the team involved. It will change your life."

Though I had done my share of traveling throughout Western and Eastern Europe, I had never considered visiting Africa and didn't know what to expect when my plane touched down at Entebbe Airport in Uganda. But as I drove through the streets of Kampala with a staff member who had volunteered to serve as my guide, I felt like I had entered a *Mad Max* sci-fi movie. The streets, most of them unpaved and full of potholes, were clogged with beat-up cars, delivery trucks, buses, bikes, pedestrians, and street kids begging for money. Half-finished buildings and decaying architecture loomed over dilapidated huts and street stands where locals hawked fruit and other goods. Uneasiness gripped me as we made our way to the guesthouse that would be my home for the next few days. My shoulder-length blond hair and light skin stuck out like a strobe light and I wasn't sure I wanted the attention.

"I'm glad I'm not alone," I admitted as we maneuvered the snarled streets. "This is definitely not Europe."

The next morning, we headed to the new primary school, situated about an hour outside of Kampala on the shores of Lake Victoria. The first few minutes of our drive was a repeat of the *Mad Max* scene from the night before. But as we neared the lake, the landscape changed so dramatically it was like entering another world. The decaying buildings and congested, crumbling roads gave way to rolling hills, dense forests, and breathtaking lake views. And when we pulled up to the primary school campus, the setting was so perfect and serene it felt like I had arrived at an exclusive retreat.

The twelve-acre campus—which held both classrooms and living accommodations for up to 150 children and staff—had been beautifully designed with carefully manicured pathways and gardens that led to the beach overlooking the lake. It was a magical oasis that had been constructed to serve some of the most destitute children in Africa.

"We want the children we serve to know that they deserve the best," my guide explained. "We want them to feel God's love."

As we talked, a sea of children rushed out to welcome us. A clamor of excited greetings rang through the air as they surrounded us and showered us with hugs.

Their joy, innocence, and love were so infectious I couldn't help but smile. They were a vacuum of positive energy that pulled in everything and everyone they surrounded.

"Come," one of the kids requested in his thick Swahili accent, "we'll show you where we live."

I was soon following the kids down a tree-lined pathway to one of several dormitories that dotted the campus. As soon as I stepped inside, I could see why the children were delighted to call this place home. The dorms, which each housed about thirty children, featured a central lounge area filled with games and books. Unlike the African outhouses I knew these children were accustomed to, the dorm had nice bathrooms and shower facilities. The best part was the children's dorm rooms, which each held six kids, with triple bunk beds, dressers, and desks.

I was impressed by the caliber of the dormitories, which featured high ceilings and exuded warmth and comfort. But what struck me most was the gratitude that emanated from my young tour guides.

"This is it," beamed one of the boys proudly, motioning to his neatly made bed. "This is where I sleep."

I spent an hour touring the classrooms and walking the campus, soaking in the beautiful, peaceful surroundings and the love and joy that radiated from every child and staff member I encountered.

From there, I was driven to the parcel of land I had funded for the new high school. The same Canadian construction firm that had built the primary school—much of it done on a volunteer basis—was now beginning the groundwork for the high school. It was impossible not to get caught up in the excitement as they walked me across the rolling hills nestled in Uganda's countryside—pausing every ten yards to explain their vision for the school. Once again, I felt like I was on the ground floor of an incredible opportunity. Only this time my anticipated return on investment was so much bigger than money. I was investing in the life-changing power of love, hope, and education.

The initial shock and unease I experienced when I first took in the Third World poverty and city chaos melted away as I began interacting with the locals. I was met with warmth and love everywhere I turned. It wasn't the automatic superficial kindness that I was used to at home. And no one I encountered seemed concerned about wasting time or being late for an appointment. What mattered was people and community.

That emphasis on relationships was driven home for me later that day, when I was taken to a hut in a nearby jungle for a home-cooked meal. I was welcomed by an elderly Ugandan woman—the grandmother of one of the schoolchildren—who treated me to the most delicious chicken and rice dish I had ever eaten. She cooked it over an open cylinder stove heated by stones. After dinner, we enjoyed papaya and mango straight off the trees and I picked my own coffee beans to take home with me.

The woman's hut was so primitive and small it could have fit in a studio apartment back home. She had so little in the way of material possessions. Yet she seemed more content than most people I knew.

I spent the next couple of days meeting with organizational leaders, touring other schools in the villages surrounding Kampala, checking out the local craft markets, and frequenting the pineapple stands that lined the city streets.

The main event during my five-day stay was the grand opening of the primary school. It was such a big celebration that journalists, government dignitaries, and even the Prime Minister of Uganda himself attended.

But it was the church service my last day there that grabbed my heart.

About a hundred children all dressed in their Sunday best gathered in a large classroom at the school with their teachers to share in the love and teachings of God.

I joined them on the small wooden benches and soaked in their voices as they sang an opening hymn. Afterward, the man leading the services directed his attention to the kids.

"Who wants to tell God what you are thankful for today?" he asked.

Before he could finish speaking, a boy around the age of ten ran to the front of the room and grabbed the wireless microphone.

"I thank Jesus that I had breakfast today," he said, radiating with gratitude.

He handed the microphone to a girl who looked to be seven or eight, now awaiting her turn.

"I'm thankful to Jesus that I am alive and that my brothers and sisters are alive," she announced.

Another boy whom I guessed to be in third grade was next in line.

"I want to thank Jesus that I get to go to school," he said.

More children had gathered at the front of the room and were patiently awaiting their turn at the microphone—all anxious to express their gratitude to Jesus for the blessings in their lives—blessings that everyone I knew from home had always taken for granted.

I could feel their words penetrating the protective wall I had erected around me, and, once inside, they acted like a healing salve, wrapping my battered insides with light and love. These children—many who had lost their parents and survived unimaginable trauma before finding their way into the school program—had every reason to be angry with the world. Instead, they radiated love, hope, and grace.

Nervous energy flooded through me as the children—who ranged from six to twelve years of age—continued to voice their thanks for their families, the loving staff, a safe place to sleep, clean clothes, and food. I had been asked to be the main speaker for the services, and though I had a strong background in theology and usually relished the opportunity to deliver a sermon, I was suddenly at a loss for words. I was used to addressing adults, not young children. I knew they had short attention spans, and after everything they had been through, I wondered what I could say that would be relevant.

Just before it was my turn to speak, an idea hit me. On the way to the podium, I grabbed a handful of dominoes from a nearby toy box and began lining them up as I spoke.

"As we go along in life we make decisions," I said as I placed the dominoes. "It's so important to make the right decisions because some of those decisions affect the rest of our lives and the lives of those around us."

I paused for a moment for effect and then knocked over the first domino, leading the entire line I had set up to fall.

That got the children's attention—which enabled me to deliver the next message I knew they needed to hear.

"It's no accident that you are all here at this school," I told them. "You are special and God has chosen you to become the future leaders of Africa."

❖

A few months later I was back in Uganda, this time accompanied by my accountant.

Max was skeptical about my donations for the land. And he was even more concerned about the money I had pledged for a new school bus.

"Why are you giving them all of that money?" he asked me every time I mentioned the school projects in Africa. "Are you sure it's legit?"

Max was a Jewish-Russian immigrant who spoke four

languages. My friends and I had affectionately nicknamed him Meyer Lansky, after the mafia's devoted accountant. I loved Max for his fierce loyalty and knew he was just trying to protect me—which is why it was so important for me that he experience for himself the power of the education initiative and the hope and love it generated. I also wanted him to experience the beauty and resilience of the children and their families. Max was going through a rough patch in his life and I knew he needed his own dose of the perspective I had gained during my last trip.

Conservative by nature, Max was determined to conduct his own due diligence to ensure my money was being put to good use and approached everything with skepticism.

At first, he wasn't even trusting of the sea of children who once again rushed out to greet me when I arrived at the primary school.

"It's all an act," he whispered under his breath as the children surrounded us and engulfed me with hugs. "They're just doing that for the donations."

His comment was so Max it almost made me laugh.

"Just wait," I said as we followed the children to their dorm so they could show off their living accommodations to him. "You'll see."

Like on my first visit, Max and I were given a comprehensive tour of the primary school campus and then taken to the site of the new high school so we could survey the progress.

Construction was now underway and as the foreman gave us a tour, showed us the building plans, and answered Max's questions, I could see a shift in his demeanor.

I noticed a gradual change in Max over the next three days as we visited with children and staff and attended the Sunday services at the school.

But it was the visit to the Kampala slum where one of the

students lived that completed his one-eighty turnaround. As we picked our way through the muddy pathway littered with rotting garbage, my thoughts traveled back to the home visit I had made six months earlier.

After my first stint in Uganda, I had headed to Kenya to experience a safari and check out an affiliate school the organization operated in Nairobi. While there I met Antanti, a father of one of the students, who worked as the security guard for the school.

We were about the same age and the two of us immediately hit it off. Like other local staff I had met, Antanti was a deeply committed Christian and the spiritual connection between us was unmistakable. He told me how grateful he was for his job at the school and said he thanked God every day that one of his children had been fortunate enough to be admitted into the school program.

As we talked, our conversation turned to life in Africa versus North America, and the vast cultural and economic differences.

"Would you like to see where I live?" he asked. "It's just across the roadway."

I had heard that Nairobi's Kibera slum, which houses more than 250,000 people, was among the worst in Africa. But nothing could have prepared me for the unthinkable misery that unfolded before me as I followed Antanti across the road that separated the haves from the have-nots.

The first thing to hit me was the stench. It was so overpowering I could almost taste the feces and urine that flowed through the filthy, open gutters. I concentrated on breathing through my mouth to block some of the smell, while, at the same time, keeping my mouth mostly closed so I wouldn't accidentally inhale a mouthful of the flies that swarmed in the sticky, humid air. Shrieks from crying children mingled with the angry barks from emaciated dogs as I carefully picked my way through the muddy, bug-infested hell, trying my best to avoid the standing water I knew was ripe with disease.

Endless rows of rundown shacks lined the muddy pathways. They all looked the same: mud walls encased in concrete with a corrugated tin roof—some without even a door.

After a twenty-minute walk that felt like a year, Antanti stopped in front of one of the shacks.

"This is it," he said, motioning me inside.

My gut felt like it was going to explode as I stepped onto the dirt floor and took in the dismal surroundings. His wife was asleep on a cot pushed up to one side of the wall. A shelf containing basic food items—oil, beans, and cornmeal—was attached to another wall. There was no bathroom or running water or stove. Just a hundred square feet of dirt covered by some mud walls and a tin roof. My thoughts flashed to Conway Kitty and his premium soft-serve cat food. I knew the cost of one can of that gourmet cat food would easily buy a week's worth of food staples for Antanti and his family, and the realization made my stomach clench.

As I took in the dire surroundings, trying to comprehend how any human being could mentally or physically survive such appalling conditions, I could feel Antanti's gaze on me.

I knew I should say something to lighten the mood—something that could offer my new friend encouragement and hope. But I was so shocked and devastated by his situation and the unfairness of it all, I was speechless.

It was Antanti who finally broke the silence.

"Randy," he said, his eyes resting on mine, "I want to tell you this because I feel the Lord wants you to know. You must have a lot of love in your heart to come to a place like this."

His words struck such an emotional chord, I had to bite the inside of my lip to stave off the tears pressing against my eyes. I was the $50 million lottery winner—the one who had everything money could buy. He lived in squalor with a dirt floor and an open sewer running behind him. Yet he was the one comforting me.

It was like he was an angel, delivering a message that God knew I desperately needed to hear.

I had been engaged in a constant battle with myself for years, questioning whether I had a loving, caring heart. I was devoted to my faith and tried hard to embody the Christian values that meant so much to me. At the same time, I knew I had a hard edge and nasty side, and I had a difficult time reconciling my dueling personalities.

As I continued to soak up Antanti's words, the weight that had been pressing down on me for years began to lift. I was surrounded by so much peace and love—and it was all emanating from my new friend.

In that moment I knew that despite his extreme poverty and destitute living conditions, Antanti was the richest man I had ever met. Antanti was overflowing with spiritual wealth that delivered happiness and well-being—something that no amount of money could buy. I knew it was the only wealth that really mattered, and I wanted it, too. It's what had prompted me to start supporting Antanti financially and what had driven me to come back to Africa and get involved with the organization in a bigger way.

Max and I were both so lost in our thoughts that neither of us spoke as we were driven back to our guesthouse for the evening. But later that night, Max told me he was so moved by everything he had experienced that he, too, wanted to get involved with the school projects.

"I get it now, Randy," he said. "I get it."

❖

Before leaving Africa, Max and I headed to the Maasai Mara Reserve in the southwest corner of Kenya to witness the migration of more than two million wildebeests, an annual event that drew spectators, photojournalists, and news media from across the world. We stood on the banks of the Mara River with the others, watching in silent awe as herds of antelope as far as the eye could see made their way toward us. We knew from our guide that crocodiles waited underwater for their prey and it wasn't long before a head popped up, locked its large jaws on one of the wildebeests, and pulled it under.

Minutes later we spotted an enormous crocodile on the other side of the river bank, about 100 feet down.

"That's the largest known crocodile in Kenya," our guide, Jerimah, said quietly. "He's over twenty-one-feet long, is wider than your arm span, and weighs more than a ton."

Only a thirty-foot-wide river and another hundred feet separated us from the jaws of one of nature's most lethal killers. The air turned electric as our group took in the giant predator.

The setup was so perfect I couldn't help myself.

"Crikey, she's a beauty," I quipped, imitating Steve Irwin, the famed TV crocodile hunter from Australia.

A group of spectators from that country caught my joke and we all burst into laughter, breaking the tension in the air.

It was surreal to be in the open wild, halfway around the world—watching animals I had only seen in zoos or on television wander freely about. I saw a lion sunning on the open savanna and giraffes taking a leisurely stroll. It was like I had been transported to a magical kingdom—so far removed from the Crawfords and my ongoing fight for justice that it seemed like a distant past.

We stayed on the reserve that evening, taking in the most stunning sunset I had ever experienced. I had always wondered why the rich lords of England in the old days would load up their trunks and head to Africa for an extended stay. Now I understood. It wasn't just one thing—it was all of it: the land, the animals, the nature, and most of all the people—who possessed the kind of love, beauty, and authenticity missing in other parts of the world.

As Max and I headed for the Nairobi Airport the following day, I thought about the talk I had been asked to give at the most recent Sunday service at the primary school in Uganda. Like my first talk, I reminded the children of God's love for them and reiterated that they were the future leaders of Africa—the doctors, engineers, teachers, pastors, and politicians who would move their continent forward.

Then, using the primary school as an analogy, I talked about the importance of having a strong foundation.

"This school is so good and solid because it was built on a good foundation," I said, eyeing the children intently. "Jesus was also a carpenter and has laid the foundation for your lives."

My first visit to Uganda had given me an initial reset. But this trip had completed my reboot. Like the children, I knew it was no fluke that I had been guided to the school program, and I now knew one of the primary purposes for my life: It was to help fund more schools so that I could provide the foundation that these kids needed to succeed.

23

Maybe I deserved the restraining order that Jeremy managed to secure against me shortly after my return from Africa. But the irony was hard to swallow.

Jeremy was the serial con artist—the one who had embezzled millions of dollars from me and had financially devastated more than a hundred others. Yet I was the one being punished.

"Are you kidding me?" I fumed as I read the order. "They won't do anything about him stealing from anyone he can get his hooks into, but they will grant him a restraining order against me for trying to stop him? What is wrong with our legal system?"

Though my personal legal battle with Jeremy was over, I had stuck to my vow to get justice for everyone who had been hurt by him. While Sandy, working in conjunction with Syd, pieced together Jeremy's fraud-ridden past for the book, I focused on the present and did everything in my power to prevent Jeremy from preying on other people.

Along with replaying my story to the media and anyone

else who would listen, I kept tabs on Jeremy's whereabouts and activities by monitoring his websites and social media posts. And I personally intervened whenever I discovered he was about to pull another con—such as notifying a potential landlord of Jeremy's tendency to skip out on rent.

But I knew it wasn't enough.

Though the Canadian news agency had exposed some of Jeremy's scams in the five articles it had published, I realized I needed a way to keep the public spotlight on his crimes. I decided to put up a website that enabled Jeremy's victims to share their stories. But Jeremy was feeling the squeeze and wasn't about to go down without a fight. He began putting out his own public messages, claiming that he was the victim in the KULTiD debacle. He even posted video footage of me he had secretly taped during the times we had spent together. Our chess game was on once again, and I was out for blood.

"You take that down now or I'm turning my attorneys on you!" I screamed into the phone. "Do it now!"

My intense anger over getting so personally betrayed by the son of a man I once considered family had sent me in a downward spiral in the days following the launch party. Shortly after discovering that KULTiD was nothing but a big con dreamed up by Jeremy to steal money—mainly from me—I shot off a volley of harassing texts to him and continued to trade occasional jabs over the next two years. Some of my comments weren't pretty. But after everything he had done to me, I figured an angry text or email here or there was fair game.

Jeremy was sending his share of nasty texts my way as well. However, he must have been saving all of mine, because the two years' worth of messages I had sent were enough for him to secure a yearlong restraining order against me that could be renewed indefinitely. And it brought all of my public whistle-blowing efforts to a screeching halt.

"We'll get this resolved in court, but, in the meantime, you need to cool it," my Canadian attorney advised. "Stay off of social media and take down the victim website until this is settled."

I spent a few days stewing. But as the weeks passed, my forced reprieve turned into a welcome break. It was like I had been given a sabbatical from an energy-sucking, high-stress job. For the first time since the KULTiD launch party, I didn't have to worry about the responsibility of taking Jeremy down. I could just relax and focus on my own life for a change. And it felt so good I started wondering if it was worth continuing my fight.

In the months following my Africa trip with Max, I had stayed in close contact with the staff overseeing the education initiative and had monitored the progress being made on the high school construction project. It was both exhilarating and gratifying to know that I was partially responsible for making the high school a reality. Just thinking about the children I had met and what the school would mean to them brought a smile to my face.

It was such a positive shift from where I had been at with Jeremy that a part of me wanted to erase the word "Crawford" from my mind and just get on with my life.

In a way it was an easy move to make because I had nothing left to prove. Along with dismantling Jeremy in court and getting back everything there was to get from him, I had finally reached a settlement with Ross Richardson, Jeremy's puppet CFO, who had paid me $500,000 for his part in the scam. What's more, after months of back and forth negotiations, I had recently sold the Scottsdale office building—completing my liquidation of all properties associated with Jeremy and the KULTiD fiasco.

I knew I could claim victory and walk away.

The only problem was that Jeremy was still on the loose, still finding a way to live it up in million-dollar houses and drive fancy sports cars, still free to steal people's money and ruin them financially and emotionally.

The knowledge that he could just keep getting away with his cons ate away at me. And after spending two years talking with people whose lives had been shattered by Jeremy, it was gnawing away at my researcher, Sandy, too.

"I never thought I would say this, but I think Jeremy is pure evil," she admitted. "Someone has got to stop him—and Amy, too."

Sandy had started her research fully expecting to encounter people who had a favorable viewpoint of Jeremy and would shed a different light on things. But no matter where she turned or who she contacted, the angry, sometimes explosive, responses were universal. And it wasn't just confined to Jeremy. It included Amy and even Dave and Shirley—who all played major roles.

I had anticipated that she would uncover more than what I already knew. But even I was taken aback by the depth and volume of Jeremy's crimes.

Through more than 100 interviews and endless hours of research that included combing through years of social media archives and blog posts, Sandy and Syd documented a life of crime and deception that spanned two decades and permeated numerous business sectors. His scams were so pervasive they read like a criminal rap sheet that extended back to his childhood—when acquaintances from that time said Jeremy would steal other children's valued possessions and then turn around and sell them to kids a few blocks away.

"It's like he was born bad," Sandy said as she detailed some of the interviews she had conducted. "It's unbelievable."

Sandy and Syd traced his business frauds back to 1998

when Jeremy, then twenty years old and newly married to Amy, launched a marketing company in Edmonton. It wasn't long before he was pocketing money earmarked for advertising space and skipping out on office rent payments. He even went as far as convincing an old high-school friend to join his staff, and then stole his identity, racking up a huge debt that included credit card charges, two Volkswagen Beetle car leases, and expensive laptops.

Having experienced it myself, it wasn't hard to understand how the employee could get so entangled in Jeremy's web of deception. The guy was a master con artist—which was amplified in the personality sketch Sandy and Syd pieced together. Everyone they interviewed described Jeremy as a charismatic, super-charged individual who combined charm and a professed devotion to God with high-pressure sales techniques and bullying tactics to get whatever he wanted. And everyone they spoke to said that what Jeremy wanted most was wealth.

After Jeremy was caught by the employee and had his hand slapped by police, Sandy and Syd discovered that he launched a magazine publishing company—mostly a scam to steal advertising dollars—which soon went out of business. In 2003, they documented that Jeremy, now living in Calgary, took his magazine con to the next level when he convinced a wealthy fellow churchgoer to put up the operating capital for the launch of a magazine called *Calgary Living Luxury Lifestyle*. He leveraged the man's business contacts to score expensive advertising contracts, drained the man's investment of more than $100,000, and then illegally pushed him out, before ensnaring other employees and advertisers in his ongoing publishing fraud.

Next came Jeremy's construction scam, which came to light for Sandy through an Edmonton man who had read the second news story and reached out to us. That scam, which Jeremy called Big West Development, drained business owners of their cash and, in some cases, left them with shoddy, half-completed construction projects. Other times, he completed the projects on the backs of the construction workers, electricians, and plumbers he hired and then skipped out on paying them by issuing worthless checks.

Sandy had started sending me sections of the meticulously documented manuscript she and Syd were writing and as I poured through the hundreds of pages of repeated cons, I could feel my insides burning. It was like reliving my nightmare over and over again.

There were so many stories of fraud and deception that it was hard to keep track of them all. But the overriding theme was the same: Jeremy would take whatever he could get, from whoever he could get it from, devastate their lives, and then relocate to another city and start looking for fresh prey.

Eventually Jeremy and Amy—working in partnership—turned to multilevel marketing (MLM), where they had access to vulnerable recruits who were entrepreneurial-minded and actively seeking out ways to improve their financial situation. Sandy and Syd uncovered numerous investment scams that ranged from telecommunications to real estate. One such scam was a lease-to-own business Jeremy called LEG Homes, in which he claimed to help anyone struggling to obtain a mortgage to get into home ownership. The scam took on various forms—and no one was immune. They found that in some cases, Jeremy would get investors to put in money for a down payment on a property and then he'd just pocket the cash without doing anything. In other cases, he used investors' money and good credit to obtain a mortgage on a property, and then kept the upfront fee and ongoing mortgage payments paid by unsuspecting customers—ultimately leaving the investor holding the bag on the mortgage and the lease-to-own customer stuck without a home. Once, Jeremy simply rented an apartment, then subleased it under the guise that it was a lease-to-own property. When he failed to pay the landlord, the tenant was evicted, leaving him homeless for three months. It was a scam I was now familiar with because Jeremy had run a version of it on the Oceanside condo in Southern California that he had secured with my investment money.

As they hopscotched from city to city and con to con, Sandy and Syd discovered that Jeremy and Amy repeatedly burned their own landlords as well. Jeremy would smooth-talk his way into a high-end lease-to-own house and then fail to make the monthly payment. The Crawfords would then squat until a forced eviction could be secured—which took longer with lease-to-own properties than with rentals.

To boost his clout among unsuspecting MLM recruits and other would-be investors, Jeremy would create a mirage of massive personal wealth, even claiming that he owned a private corporate jet and had purchased a home for Dave and Shirley using his MLM earnings. Dave amped up the deception, making social media comments about his son's new jet and appearing in an MLM video—produced by Jeremy—expressing his gratitude for the home his son had purportedly bought him and Shirley. In reality, it was just another Crawford rental that would again go unpaid.

My insides felt like they had been tossed into a food processor and were now being ground into bits as I continued to read the manuscript. There was so much pain in these pages, so many lives that had been destroyed by Jeremy, Amy, Dave, and Shirley—and yet they continued to get a free pass. It was like every fraud they committed was a building block that led to yet a bigger, more pervasive fraud. And it had all culminated with KULTiD, which had ensnared more than a dozen unsuspecting investors prior to my involvement and had netted millions of dollars that benefited the entire Crawford clan.

It was so infuriating I wanted to hunt down Jeremy and Amy, slap some handcuffs on them, and lock them up myself. But given the restraining order, a citizen's arrest was out of the question. And beyond the futility of it, I no longer had the energy to keep my vigilante fight going.

My attorney was still working to get the restraining order lifted so I could ensure that Sandy and Syd's book—which I was financially supporting—would make it out into the world. I hoped that it would bring validation and healing to some of the victims and generate the exposure necessary to at least keep Jeremy, Amy, and the rest of the Crawfords from hurting others. But I figured that was as much as I could do.

I was now six months into the restraining order and the rage that had fueled my internal flame was gone—in fact, most days I felt light and happy. I was spending more time at my log-cabin house with Conway, and I enjoyed long hours with a mug of coffee on my wraparound deck while soaking up the sun and the beauty of my peaceful, wooded surroundings.

That's what I was doing when Syd's phone call came.

"Randy, I think we've got Jeremy on securities fraud," he announced, his tone cautious but excited. "There are no guarantees, but from what I've uncovered, I think we've got a good case for the Alberta Securities Commission."

Before I had a chance to absorb his words, Syd began explaining how he had stumbled upon his discovery. While doing research for the KULTiD chapter of the book, he noticed that most of the scammed investors had been issued shares of bogus stock in the company by Jeremy. Out of curiosity, Syd said he began looking into securities fraud and realized he had hit pay dirt.

"I started reading case law and found that what Jeremy did

are more than minor infractions. They are serious."

A twinge of excitement shot through me as Syd continued talking. He told me that nearly everything Jeremy had done in relation to issuing shares was against the law.

It started with the shareholders agreement itself, which Syd said was supposed to provide a detailed, accurate snapshot of the company. Instead, the document Jeremy provided was packed with lies.

They were so over-the-top they even seemed a stretch for Jeremy. Among other things, he claimed that the KULT team was comprised of the "most sought-after security, software, and technology experts."

The private offering memorandum also claimed that KULT's "revolutionary technologies are being applied in the fields of Digital Content Management, Branding Intelligence Data, Content Security, Trend Monitoring, Financial Transaction Security, Cloud Commerce Systems and Personal Mobile Communication Security," and said that "KULTiD is the de facto standard in cross platform content marketing and management for the world's largest brands and brand systems."

If that wasn't enough, Syd said he had learned that Jeremy made all of the investors—even those who barely knew him or had never met him at all—check the Friends and Family box on the required government forms, enabling him to circumvent certain reporting requirements. According to the investors involved, Jeremy told them this was just how it was done and made it a condition of investing with him.

What's more, Syd said Jeremy never signed the share agreements, which is also required by law. On top of that, Syd told me he uncovered some cases where shares were issued before KULT was even incorporated. And in my case, he had actually gone as far as issuing me shares that had already been issued to someone else. This was something I had already known about, but had written off as just another aspect of Jeremy's cons.

"They are all serious violations, and when you put them together, it shows a continuous pattern of fraud—which is what the Alberta Securities Commission looks for," Syd explained.

"Sandy and I have collected affidavits and shareholder documentation from a dozen investors who have agreed to join the shared complaint we are filing," he added. "But we need your help. We need you to join the complaint and provide your documentation because your investment represents eighty percent of the money Jeremy stole and will give it the big-dollar value that we hope will get the Securities Commission's attention."

Syd's words were like a gust of wind on a smoldering flame. I could feel the fire once again roaring inside of me. Only this time it wasn't a rage-fueled fire—it was fueled by a newfound hope that justice would finally be served. And it was accompanied by the sense of peace that came with knowing that between Sandy, Syd, and myself, we had done everything in our power to prevent Jeremy and Amy from hurting others.

Jeremy might have temporarily stopped me from posting public comments about him on websites or social media, or sharing stories of his crimes with the world. But there was nothing preventing me from providing Syd with the documentation he needed to deliver his case to the Alberta Securities Commission.

It had never occurred to me that it would be Jeremy's fraudulent shareholder offerings to me and a dozen other KULT investors that could finally do him in. But I was thrilled to turn over my documents and sign the shared complaint with others.

Maybe, finally, the legal system would kick into gear and do the right thing.

"Okay, Syd, here's what you do," I said as I delivered the

signed documents. "Take everything you have, spell it out, and package it up with a neat little bow for them. If that doesn't do it, I don't know what will. But at least we can say we did everything we could."

24

It was as though I had just woken up from my own Wizard of Oz dream. And it felt so good I wanted to shout it to the world.

"I'm back!" I announced to Conway, who was curled up in his familiar resting place against my head. "I'm back."

Nearly three and a half years had passed since that frigid Saturday morning trip to the Lamont corner grocer to fetch Conway his premium soft-serve cat food. In some ways that was like another lifetime and I knew a piece of that old me was gone. But the essence of my old self had reemerged from the wild rocket ride intact. It was such a welcome relief I was ready to break out into a happy dance.

The intense endorphin high that had me shooting through space and hopping from one country or continent to another was gone. I could breathe normally again and was once again sleeping at night. I was even starting to crack jokes and laugh again—something my friends immediately noticed.

"Dude, your sense of humor is back," one of them remarked

during a recent barbeque, prompting the others to chime in.

For the first time since my lottery win, everything in my life felt right. Though I still took occasional trips and spent an odd night or two at my ocean view condo, I now considered my log cabin home. I loved the open space, the woods that surrounded it, the sound of the river that bordered the property. I loved the smell of the cedar and the feel of Conway making his presence known by brushing against my leg or curling up beside me. And more than anything, I loved the peace and solitude it provided.

After being trapped in a never-ending Indy 500 race, I had finally figured out how to let my foot off the gas pedal and was giving myself the time and space I needed to reflect on my life. It was a journey that conjured so many emotions it was hard to separate and process them all. I could hear the voice repeating the question in my mind, trying to solve a puzzle that made no logical sense: How did a welfare kid with an absent, criminal dad who had been murdered and a struggling teen mom who had her own demons to battle end up with a pile of money so massive it was hard to comprehend?

As a kid, I had never expected my life to amount to much. All my early male role models were small-time crooks and thugs who rotated in and out of jail, and by the time Steve married my mom and moved us to a more stable environment, my path seemed to be set.

I had emerged as the class clown with a big personality and a wild streak who struggled to read and sucked at school. I figured I would end up being a truck driver or working in a wood mill—assuming I lived to see adulthood.

And even after I had cleaned up my affairs, found God and decided to pursue a life in the ministry, my future looked dismal.

My chest ached each time I thought of my twenty-six-year-old self standing on that bridge in the black of night—so destitute and full of despair over my failed life quest and inability to land any sort of a job that I considered jumping to my death to end the pain.

I was now fifty-two, exactly twice the age of when I almost took my life. What if I had done it? And what did it mean that I was still here—and blessed with virtually everything I could imagine wanting: close friends, a loyal cat, a beautiful house, and all the security money could buy?

It was a reality I wrestled with because I was a scrapper who had always had to fight and work so hard for everything I had ever gotten. I had managed to pull myself together that night on the bridge and claw my way out of the abyss, eventually finding my way into sales and leveraging the one gift I had been given—the ability to connect with anyone I met—to become one of the most successful sales reps at Hertz. Achieving a salary that topped $200,000 a year had seemed like a lot at the time. But it was a far cry from the $50 million I had been handed and it was hard to shake the guilt that came with knowing that I didn't earn it. It was a self-destructive mindset Derek was working to squash.

"Did you do anything illegally to get it?" He pushed when I expressed my feelings to him. "Did you rob a bank or push over an old woman? No, right? You got it legally and it's yours."

Like my emotions, my reflections were scattered—jumping from one memory and incident to the next. Maybe it was this underlying guilt that had been partially to blame for landing me in the mess with Jeremy.

My mind replayed the meticulously mental preparations I had made in the years leading up to my big win. I was convinced I had it all planned out, that I had safeguarded myself from any problems by getting out of town and having Lisa take over my bills and finances. But I had overlooked the emotional factor.

I hadn't accounted for the cracks that came with loving and trusting people such as Dave Crawford. Nor had I realized that my intense internal drive to succeed wouldn't go away just because I had $50 million deposited in my bank account. If anything, it had amplified my need to prove that I was worthy of that kind of gift.

If I could push a rewind button I would go back to my first day at the Ocean Promenade Hotel three weeks after my lottery win, cut myself off from the world and live out my plan to take a year off from any decisions. It would have kept me from getting sucked into Jeremy's KULT scam and saved me years of legal battles. It would have also prevented me from throwing myself into other business ventures such as the septic system debacle.

This, too, was something Derek was helping me to work through.

"It was bound to happen, Randy," he stressed. "But now you've been through it, have learned from it, and have made it to the other side."

He was right about that: I had definitely learned some hard lessons. I learned—as Derek had warned from the beginning—that friends and business don't mix. I learned that big-dollar business investments weren't my strong suit—that I was a visionary—not a day-to-day operations guy, and that I needed to surround myself with trusted professionals like Derek and Max to guide me with my finances. I also learned that when it came to giving, I needed to have firm boundaries in place.

My internal walls had definitely gone up after the Crawford nightmare. But it wasn't just them. It was other people close to me constantly hitting me up for money—acting like it was theirs.

Two of the most painful instances centered around my mom and my long-time friend, Brent.

My mom and I had been estranged for more than two years when I hit the lottery jackpot and the money, as I feared it might, only drove a further wedge between us. Her sense of entitlement was so great that my stepdad, whom I financially supported through expensive experimental cancer treatments in Mexico, expressed anger that I hadn't broken off $10 million of my winnings for them. And though I had given them several hundred thousand dollars over a three-year period and provided them with a free place to live in a house I had purchased in Ottawa, nothing I did was enough. In the end, our already strained relationship deteriorated so much that my mom didn't even invite me to my stepdad's recent funeral.

Then there was Brent and his wife, Kim. Though both earn good salaries as senior officers with the Royal Canadian Mounted Police, they constantly hit me up for cash. I had paid off a $125,000 debt they owed when I first came into my money. And when they came to me eight months later with another $80,000 debt—using the cost of raising triplets as an excuse—I wiped that out, too. Like Dave Crawford and my parents, I had also given them a free place to live in a million-dollar house and required only that they pay the utilities. But they kept coming back for more and when I finally drew the line and said I was done being their personal bank, they became livid.

"What's it to you?" Kim spouted angrily. "You've got plenty of money. It's not like it's going to hurt you any."

When the situation reached a boiling point and I asked them to leave my house, they thanked me by leaving it trashed. The house I had so joyously tracked down with Kim's help two and a half years earlier so I could make her and Brent's life easier was in such disrepair that it ultimately cost $150,000 to get it back into its original condition.

I had always been generous with my money—always tried

to give what I could to help those in need. But now I was being viewed as an unlimited ATM machine for anyone who wanted cash, and I was tired of being used.

In the years since my lottery win, I'd been bombarded with financial requests. Sometimes they were in the form of emails from old friends' wives who swore that their husbands didn't know that they were reaching out, but claimed that they were in desperate need of money.

Some people contacted me requesting a new vehicle. Others wanted money to pay their bills. Still others just said they could use an infusion. One recent request came from Brent's friend, Dan, who wanted me to co-sign on his mortgage so he wouldn't lose his house. It was the third time he had contacted me for financial help in the last year and I was fed up.

"As a co-signer, I will be liable if you default," I replied. "I can't be the go-to guy because of people's financial delinquency or mismanagement skills!

"You have a PhD and are a very bright guy," I added before blocking him from my email account. "You're not some person who has lost his family to war or famine."

I was now clear on my giving priorities and it centered on making life better for destitute children around the world, which is where my heart had been from the start. I had recently donated more money to the high school project in Uganda and was now thinking about my long-term legacy. I loved the African education initiative because of its lasting positive impact and was starting to envision the construction of a new, world-class university there that I could help spearhead down the road.

I now realized that my money was best spent helping those who were devoted to helping others—people like the British woman I recently met who had walked away from a lucrative career to serve as a teacher for vulnerable children in Gambia.

"So how much does it cost to educate a child for a year?" I asked her as I drove her around Vancouver, giving her a quick tour of the city she was visiting.

"A hundred pounds," she replied.

My head buzzed as I calculated the numbers. A hundred pounds amounted to roughly $125 (in US dollars). For $5,000 USD, I could provide an education for forty children for a year.

The amount of $5,000 just popped into my mind—an amount I was inspired to give. I knew that money would bring joy to both the teacher and the children it helped. And knowing that brought me joy, too.

That's one of the biggest lessons I had learned since my lottery win: Long-term happiness had nothing to do with stuff—it was about making a positive difference in the world.

I had gone a little crazy, had been the pig at the smorgasbord—but the days of wild excess were over. In the year and a half since I had sold the Ferrari to fund the high school project, I had liquidated half of my car collection and now made sure that any cars I purchased were a sound business investment.

I wanted to enjoy the money, but I knew now I didn't need expensive toys to experience joy—something that was driven home for me during a recent exchange with a wealthy friend.

He was as passionate about boats as I was about cars and had flown to England to check out a yacht he had his eye on—a fifty-five-foot floating estate that came with a steep price tag. While there, he also checked out an eighty-foot yacht, which sold for an even steeper price tag.

"Maybe we should go in on it together, Randy," he pitched over text. "Between the two of us, we can swing it with no problem."

The Randy of a year earlier would have seriously entertained the idea. But now a purchase that extravagant was so far out of my realm of consciousness that the suggestion was almost comical.

"This is a test, right?" I replied, laughing as I typed the words.

As I continued to reflect on my journey, my thoughts locked on Jeremy. I was now nine months into his restraining order, and I felt so much peace and contentment I almost wanted to write him a thank-you card.

I had let go of the anger and pain I had carried inside of me and was allowing everything to take its course. Syd and Sandy had sent the documentation regarding Jeremy's securities fraud to the Alberta Securities Commission and had received confirmation that the package had arrived. They had also sent a document more than 400 pages long detailing Jeremy and Amy's serial cons to the Royal Canadian Mounted Police, who had, in turn, referred them to the Calgary Police.

"This falls in their jurisdiction," the police officer they spoke with explained. "But we have opened a file on Jeremy and Amy and your document is in there. They are now on our radar."

I wasn't sure where the criminal case would lead. But the same energy that had been building in me prior to my lottery win was once again building and I knew things were closing in on Jeremy. The restraining order he had fought to keep in place against me indefinitely was set to end on February 1, 2020. And I planned to release Sandy and Syd's book to the world as soon as it lifted.

Calm washed over me as I thought about the tidal wave headed Jeremy and Amy's way. I was initially apprehensive of the court hearing I had been required to attend in conjunction with the restraining order the previous month. I had done a lot of healing in the time since the restraining order had first gone into effect and I worried that seeing Jeremy and Amy would reignite the rage and resentment. But I experienced none of that when I saw them in court. I didn't even feel it when Jeremy—who was acting as his own legal representative because yet another attorney had called it quits on him—asked me questions.

I was so detached it was like I was a spectator watching the scene unfold. But as the court proceedings wore on, a thought formed in my mind that I couldn't shake: How could this be the guy who took me for millions and caused me so much grief?

Jeremy didn't look like a man who had swindled more than a hundred people out of millions of dollars. He looked exhausted and beaten down—as did Amy.

Maybe it was an act, but I could hear the cracks in his voice when he told the judge he had no way to pay his legal fees and could feel the heaviness that permeated both him and Amy. And that's when it hit me. Maybe it didn't matter if they ended up rotting behind bars. Maybe exposing Jeremy and Amy to the world and turning them into public pariahs was worse than jail. That public exposure would be Dave and Shirley's fate as well.

I had originally planned to drag them through the court system, go after every nickel and dime I could get and, at the very least, get back pay for the nine months they spent squatting in my Sherwood Park house. But I had dropped my lawsuit against them earlier in the year—no longer interested in devoting my energy to them. They knew what they did, and God knew what they did. And they would have to live with that.

Somewhere along my journey over the past few months, I had realized that if I wanted true happiness in my life, I had to let go of the hate and the hurt and disengage with any toxic people.

That's where I was now—free of the toxic waste I had been metabolizing for so long. From a mental perspective, my life was a clean slate and I couldn't wait to figure out my next act.

The possibilities were endless. I had the financial security, time and freedom to do anything I wanted with my life. I wasn't sure what it was yet, but I knew I wanted it to be something that tapped into my creative juices. Maybe I would start a writing group with my friends so we could capture some of our stories and humor on paper. Or maybe we would start a comedy act. My friends were by far the funniest guys I had ever met and among the group of us, I knew we could come up with something good. Maybe I would even make a documentary or get into movie production. There were so many great stories out there just waiting to be told. Or maybe I would design T-shirts or build custom bird houses.

That was the beauty of it. I could pursue anything I wanted to pursue. It was energizing just thinking about the possibilities. I was in no hurry, though. I was still in recuperation mode and was taking the time to just be and think and enjoy life. Since settling into my log-cabin house, I had been focusing on the simple pleasures—the ones that didn't require a big bank account. What I enjoyed most now was what I had enjoyed most pre-lottery win—hanging out and laughing with my friends, or kicking back in front of the TV with Conway and a fresh-brewed cup of dark roast coffee.

That's what Conway and I were doing now—only instead of watching TV, we were out on the wraparound deck, soaking up a beautiful summer morning. I loved being back with Conway on a regular basis. It was like coming home. I'm not sure what Conway thought about the whirlwind ride of the last three and a half years, or if he even understood that anything had changed. But what I knew for certain was that I didn't have to question Conway's motives. His love and loyalty for me were unconditional—at least as long as I kept his bowl full of his premium soft-serve cat food. And I felt that same love and loyalty for him. Our setting may have changed, but we were right back to where we started—just the two of us, enjoying a lazy morning together.

Thinking about the cat food and Conway and the hungry, angry meows that led to my lottery win discovery made me laugh.

If only Conway knew what a celebrity he was. It was a reality I had been reminded of eight months earlier, when I took a quick trip to Edmonton to meet with my attorneys.

We had just finished dinner and had stepped out into the freezing cold—waiting for the street light to turn so we could make a beeline to the warmth of our car.

As we stood at the corner, a group of women came up behind us. I could hear them chatting ad laughing among themselves. Then one of the women motioned to me.

"Oh, my gosh, that's him!" she exclaimed in an excited tone.

Though I had grown out my hair as a partial disguise, I was still recognized from time to time because of the media coverage following my win, and I could sense the anticipation building as I waited for her to say my name.

Instead, I was swiftly put in my place.

"That's the guy," she exclaimed again, her voice louder and more animated. "That's Conway Kitty's owner."

Epilogue

January 2019

From an economic perspective, the Sudanese refugee camps scattered along the northwest border of Uganda weren't in as dire circumstances as those I'd encountered during my visit to the Kibera slum in Nairobi two years earlier.

Unlike the open sewers that ran through Kibera, there was basic sanitation in the form of outhouses that dotted the settlement camps. Though there was no running water, the refugees had been issued yellow water jugs that could be filled with fresh drinking water from the water trucks that made weekly rounds to the various settlements. And instead of the endless rows of dilapidated ten-by-ten-foot shacks that clogged the Kibera slum, the Sudanese refugees lived in mud-brick huts that each came with a tiny plot of land for gardening.

Yet the heaviness of the emotional baggage and trauma that permeated the refugee camps was so much worse. Because unlike the residents of Kibera, who had grown up there and accepted it as their way of life, the Sudanese refugees had been forced into these camps. They had been forced to flee their country, their homes, and their careers. And they had endured unimaginable terror along the way.

One of the men who had accompanied me on the seven-hour journey into the refugee camps showed me the deep scars from the bullet holes that had riddled his arms and torso as he fled from warring tribes. Another recounted how his entire family had been ambushed and slaughtered while driving home from a wedding. He had escaped the same fate only because he had chosen to stay home that day. Later he'd managed to flee to the safety of Northern Uganda. The emotional pain and trauma of both men was mirrored on the faces of every refugee I met that day and was so tangible I could feel it in my bones.

"It reminds me of my trip to Rwanda after the genocide," explained the African director for the education organization I was working with. "I've never seen such blank-looking people. They had experienced so much trauma and horror that they were broken.

"These are proud people who were bookkeepers and teachers and government officials in their old lives in Southern Sudan," she continued. "They've lost everything and have endured so much trauma, and now they have to live in these settlement camps and are told that they have to be farmers. It's emotionally devastating."

Two days later, while still processing everything I had seen and heard, I was seated in a Christian radio station in Northern Uganda, where I had been invited to speak. My host told me I would be reaching several million people throughout Southern Sudan, Uganda, and the Congo. I knew I needed to say something that would foster hope and healing and also remind the refugees that they had not been forsaken by God.

"You know, Moses and Abraham and Noah were all refugees," I started, referring to the Old Testament to drive home my message. "Mohammad and Buddha were also refugees. A lot of great men in history were refugees. Through their struggles, they gained wisdom and rose to greatness, and it's their words and teachings that we now turn to for solace and guidance. As difficult as it is, to have this experience really shows the heart of God."

While I spoke, my words were translated for the radio audience and I could see the nods of approval from my radio hosts. It was a heavy subject but I could feel the energy around me lifting as I spoke, and when they invited me to return to deliver more sermons, I knew I would be back.

As I relaxed in my room at a nearby guesthouse that evening, I reflected on my experiences over the past two weeks. It was my third trip to Africa in two years, and I had kicked off my trip to Kenya by visiting people I now considered close friends. While there, I made the trek to an outreach school on the Masara plain run by a mother and daughter. I had formed a bond with the two women during my first visit and always stopped by to say hi and provide some financial assistance for the school. But I also had another reason for my visit: the two resident cats I had nicknamed Skinny and Scrawny. The cats came running when they saw me.

"How are my two buddies?" I murmured as I buried my hands in their fur and then filled their bowls with the cat food I had brought. "You know I would never forget about the two of you."

Peace washed over me as I soaked in the quiet of my room, thinking about my journey over the past few years. Though it felt like a natural progression, it was crazy to think that I was once again hanging out in Africa and that this was actually my life. Four years into my lottery win, I was finally gaining my footing. I had spent Christmas with friends in Northern Ireland, soaking in the beauty and wonder of that country. I was so firm on my commitment to take a year off to just be and think that I had already rented a house in Europe for a few months in the spring. Though I was still figuring out my personal life, I knew it involved a bigger role in Africa. Thanks to the open invitation at the radio station and invitations to speak at local churches, I was getting back to my roots as a minister—that career I had dreamed of as a twenty-something. Only now, thirty years later, I finally had the life experiences necessary to counsel and inspire others. From a philanthropy perspective, my vision was also beginning to take shape.

My trip had included a stop in Kampala for a status update on the high school I was helping to support in Uganda. The school was now nearing completion and while they were finishing the interior, they were beginning to focus on staffing needs.

Just thinking about the school and what it would mean to African youth in the years to come was exhilarating. I could feel my excitement building as I voiced my thoughts for the future to the director who oversaw all African education projects.

"Let's get this high school up and running and fully established," I told her. "Then let's look at building a college to train people for a career in the trades or to prepare them for university.

"And once that is going strong, let's build a world-class university," I added, giving voice to the idea that had been brewing in my mind.

I knew it was a big dream. But, like my lottery win, I could visualize it clearly. And if I could leave a legacy of a high school, a college, and a university over the next thirty years, maybe I could say I had done something worthwhile with my life.

Crawford Update

April 2019

I WAS RELAXING IN NORTHERN IRELAND in late March when I received a phone call from a sergeant at the Alberta Securities Commission.

He explained that he had recently transferred to the Securities Commission from the RCMP and had come across a large file on Jeremy Crawford containing the extensive documentation that Syd and Sandy had sent nearly a year earlier.

"I want to hear your story," he said. "When can we talk face to face?"

I could feel the energy surging through me as I considered his request. Getting the attention of law enforcement and convincing them they had to act was what I had been fighting for ever since I had realized I was dealing with a serial con artist. But I was now in such a good place emotionally, I wondered if I wanted to subject myself to it all over again.

Even as I contemplated that thought, though, I knew I would.

"Name the time and I will be there," I replied.

A few weeks later I was in the offices at the Alberta Securities Commission in Calgary, sharing my story with the sergeant. I could feel myself once again heating up as I recounted how Jeremy—working in cahoots with Amy, Dave, and Shirley—had conned me out of $4.6 million. I told him about the six months leading up to the November 1 launch party, when the full extent of the fraud came crashing down around me. Then I detailed the eight-month court battle that ensued—with Jeremy's blatant disregard of court orders and the contempt of court rulings that dragged on for most of the case. I also relayed my attorney's discovery that, along with embezzling money from the company, he and Amy had evaded taxes in both the US and Canada. During my four-hour deposition, I also talked about the dozens of Crawford victims who had contacted me after my court case hit the national media, and I shared some of their heartbreaking stories. I wrapped up my account by noting that, during their research, Syd and Sandy had uncovered more than a hundred people whose lives had been devastated by the Crawfords.

"This is a complicated case," the sergeant agreed when I had finished speaking. "It's going to take some time to investigate."

Hearing the sergeant say that Jeremy was officially under investigation awoke something inside of me. The same steely resolve that had driven me to expose the Crawfords and get justice for every person who had been hurt by them was once again kicking in. But now it wasn't just the Crawfords that I wanted to stop.

As I left the deposition, it hit me that I now knew exactly what I was supposed to be doing with my life. Along with my ongoing philanthropic work in Africa, I knew it was my calling to spearhead the fight against white-collar crime.

"It's one of the ways I'm going to use my platform," I told Max a few days later. "You were right. Taking down the

Crawfords and other white-collar criminals is a big reason I've been gifted with this money."

Stopping White-Collar Crime: I Need Your Help

I'm determined to shine the public spotlight on white-collar crime and ensure that anyone who commits these crimes is brought to justice. But I can't do it alone. If you have been the victim of a white-collar crime or know someone who has, please report it to the police and spread the word. Please also share your story on my website: www.randall-rush.com.

Together, we can put an end to this.

Appendix

KULT Labs Corp.
Scottsdale, AZ

U.S. Consulate General
Toronto, Ontario
Canada

August 27, 2015

Re: **Petition for Nonimmigrant E-2 Visa Worker**
    Petitioner: KULT Labs Corp.
    Beneficiary: Jeremy D. Crawford.

Dear Sir or Madam:

We write this letter in support of our E-2 visa petition, submitted herewith, on behalf of Mr. Jeremy D. Crawford. We are seeking to employ Mr. Crawford in E-2 status for a five-year period in a specialty occupation as a Chief Executive Officer. To this end, we have taken the liberty of detailing below the nature of our business as well as the professional position which Mr. Crawford will hold, and his qualifications.

The Petitioner.

KULT Labs Corp. is located in Scottsdale, AZ. KULT Labs Corp. works in the software development industry. The Company plans on rolling out the KULTiD.com Corp. product to the public in the fourth quarter of 2015.

The Position.

The position being offered to Mr. Crawford is that of Chief Executive Officer. Mr. Crawford's duties and responsibilities will include the following: 1) leading the development and execution of the Company's long term strategy with a view to create shareholder value; 2) responsible for all day-to-day management decisions and for implementing the Company's long and short term plans; 3) ensure the Company is appropriately organized and staffed.

KULT 000076

KULT Labs E-2 Visa Petition on behalf of Jeremy Crawford, dated August 27, 2015.

For more information and to view legal documentation regarding the many cons and crimes of Jeremy Crawford, please visit www.jercrawfraud.com.

The Beneficiary.

Mr. Crawford is well qualified for the position offered. He has over 16 years of Marketing Experience selling advertising and marketing products to his clients. He was the founding Publisher of Edmonton Style Magazine, Calgary Living Magazine, Alberta Oil Magazine and Toronto Elite Magazine. He was also the Director of Publication Development and Associate Publisher of Privilege Magazine in Toronto. Jeremy has led the passion for designing and developing digital products into the mobile wallet space. He has successfully developed the next platform in taking interest in product through social media and creating purchase seamless transactions. Jeremy has created personal high performance production courses to teach individuals with little or no business experience how to perform. He has a proven track record for success in many companies he has worked closely with. We believe Mr. Crawford possesses the unique qualifications in the area of the software development industry that we require for the offered position. For his professional services, Mr. Crawford will be compensated at a salary of $330,000.00. a year. This wage rate is within the prevailing wage for similar positions and will not adversely affect the working conditions of similarly employed U.S workers. Further, if KULT Labs Corp. terminated Mr. Crawford's services prior to the expiration of his E-2 status, we will compensate him for his return trip to his country of nationality.

We look forward to receiving your approval of this application as soon as possible

Yours truly,

Ross Richardson
Chief Financial Officer

KULT Labs Corp.
8712 E. Vista Bonita Dr.
Scottsdale, AZ 85255

KULT 000077

Book Club Questions

1. In what ways has Randy been lucky in his life? In what ways has he not been lucky? How do you think Randy would define "luck" at the end of the book?

2. Why does Conway Kitty matter to the memoir?

3. Randy "bucked the odds" all his life. Discuss.

4. What kinds of faith does this book depict?

5. Do you think Randy's close circle of friends were, in his eyes, his family?

6. Was the betrayal by Dave Crawford made worse by his being a main of faith? A father figure? Do you think betrayal by another friend would have affected Randy as much?

7. Randy had a plan for how to handle winning the lottery. He didn't follow it. Why do you think he changed his mind? Would you do the same, in a similar circumstance?

8. Why do you think some lottery winners struggle after winning? Do you think lotteries are a good thing?

9. In what ways does Randy transform by the end of the book?

10. Randy is using his lottery winnings to support educational programs in Africa. Do you think all lottery winners should support charities? What charities would you support if you won the lottery and why?

11. Have you ever dreamed of winning the lottery? Having read Randy's account of his experience, would you handle winning differently than you might have before knowing Randy's story?

12. Why do you think Randy decided to expose the Crawfords? What do you know about white collar crime? Do you believe it is taken as seriously as other kinds of crime? What do you think Randy hopes his efforts will achieve?

Acknowledgments

When I first started this project I wanted it to be a very inspirational book that would give people a glimmer of hope in the midst of very severe life circumstances. Whether good or bad—oh, how quickly life can change! Still, if my own experience has taught me anything, it's that hard work and perseverance always pays off in the end. People do win the lottery, I guess... When it happens to you, well, it's a ride, to say the least. When it happens to you, you find out fast who your real friends and family are—really, really fast.

This book is the result of a lot of hard work from Ingrid Ricks. Working with her throughout this project, amidst the personal health struggles she has soldiered through all the while, has been one of the most inspirational experiences of my life. I dedicate this work to her spirit of perseverance and devotion to her profession.

I would also like to thank all the characters in this book,

whether heroes or villains. It is all of these cocktails of life experiences coupled with the personalities I have encountered on my journey that has forged who I am today, and who I will become as I continue to venture down the road of life. I would also like to acknowledge not just the people who have walked parts of this path with me, but also the very special animals I have had in my life that and with whom I have shared so many amazing stories and experiences that are not included in this book.

And, ultimately, I would like to thank the Lord—who has been with me through both the highs and lows—for a very privileged life.

About the Author

Randy Rush is on a mission of social good to stop white-collar crime and other social injustices by exposing them to the world. He founded Rantanna Media, a social good publishing and media company, to give victims a voice and raise widespread awareness about the devastating impact of these crimes and other social injustices. Randy devotes time and resources to the foundations he creates to help those in need. Randy is especially committed to transforming the lives of children in Africa by providing them the education, love and hope they need to succeed.

He divides his time between Canada and Europe. For more information, visit www.RandyRushSpeaks.com.

Other Books by Randy Rush

Bloodsuckers

"Have nothing to do with the 'stinky fish' Jeremy Crawford."

Fifty-million-dollar lottery winner Randy Rush was only out for personal justice when he launched a court battle against Jeremy Crawford, a skilled con man who exploited mutual relationships and a deeply devoted Christian facade to swindle him out of more than $4.6 million.

But that all changed when Rush's court case hit Canada's national news media and other Crawford victims began contacting him to share their own stories of financial and emotional devastation.

Stunned by the volume of criminal accusations and outraged by lax laws when it comes to white collar crime, Rush realized that the only way to stop Jeremy, his wife, Amy, and his parents, Dave and Shirley, from hurting others was to expose them to the world.

In this scathing exposé, *Bloodsuckers*, Rush — working with a team of researchers — documents Jeremy and Amy Crawfords' twenty-year crime spree ranging from identity theft to embezzlement to securities fraud. The book is based on more than a hundred interviews, countless hours of research and thousands of pages of meticulously documented records kept by victims who have held onto them over the years — hoping that the information would one day take the Crawfords down.

After years of suffering in silence, *Bloodsuckers* gives victims the opportunity to finally have their voices heard. In doing so, it spotlights the devastating impact of white-collar crime and the glaring need for our criminal justice system to take action and do more to protect the public from these life-destroying criminals.

Bloodsuckers is available worldwide. Purchase on Amazon or via www.randall-rush.com.

CPSIA information can be obtained
at www.ICGtesting.com
Printed in the USA
BVHW030553130223
658285BV00004B/950